NO TIME OUT FROM GRIEF

SURVIVING THE DEATH OF MY SON

Terri Huber
Poetry by John Huber

Writers Club Press
San Jose · New York · Lincoln · Shanghai

No Time Out From Grief

ISBN: 0-595-00076-2

Published by Writers Club Press, an imprint of iUniverse.com, Inc.

For information address:
iUniverse.com, Inc.
620 North 48th Street
Suite 201
Lincoln, NE 68504-3467
www.iuniverse.com

URL: http://www.writersclub.com

Dedicated to

Alex & Morgan
Our two sons
"One with us and one waiting for us"
All of our love, forever.

Mom & Dad

TABLE OF CONTENTS

FOREWORD

In this book, Terri tells the story of a journey that no parent wishes to take—a journey of a parent's survival after the death of their child. When our eighteen-year-old son, Erik, died we joined Terri on this journey. She was one of The Compassionate Friends that met us at our first group meeting. To us, she was already far down the path and someone that we followed to gain back our strength and stability.

Little did we know the depth and breadth of her sorrow and the difficult road that each of us must travel to survive. Both of us feel that Terri's dedication to Compassionate Friends made a huge difference in our lives. She made us feel welcome in a place and time where none of us wanted to be. People like Terri and the other Compassionate Friends gave us the courage to forge ahead for another minute, hour, day, month, and now, years.

We are currently co-leaders of the Portland Chapter of The Compassionate Friends. We hear the stories of many bereaved parents, each as unique as the children they are grieving. Yet, each path has similarities. In this book, Terri tells her story, which is unique and yet similar to our own and others.

We believe that bereaved parents, as well as those wishing to comfort those parents, can benefit from reading her story. If you are a bereaved parent, this story will offer you hope. If you know a bereaved parent, this story will give you insight into feelings that you may find difficult to comprehend. Terri shares her feelings of disbelief, anger, despair, depression, and finally, hope. Everyone who loses a child knows these feelings. Even Terri's thoughts of her own death are not unknown to those in deep depression. Each of us in our own way has to reconcile why we are still living and why we should continue to live.

There is not a *right way* to grieve and each of us must travel our own journey. Some of us turn to our faith, some to family, some to friends and some to professionals. Like Terri, many of us have found tremendous support from The Compassionate Friends. The friends that we find at TCF meetings, along with bereaved parents who struggle on alone, are the only people who can really say, "We know how you feel."

This story will also give you an insight into the timeline of grief. Too many people feel that *you'll get over it* and after as little as a year inquire, "Why are you still crying?" It is hard for others to comprehend that the grief caused by the loss of a child does not go away. Most of us learn to control it but grief remains with us.

Terri shares her search for "the magic wand" that *would* make it all better, as she too believed that the pain would end if she could just find the right way to do it. She discovered there is no right way, though, only a process of one step at a time through the quagmire of grief.

Terri, you and Alex are an inspiration. We feel that you are a blessing and a gift to this world from God. Thank you for being part of our lives.

With love and compassion,

Lynetta and Chuck Weswig

Co-Leaders of the Portland, Oregon Chapter of The Compassionate Friends

"If something happened to one of my children, I would just die!" Famous last words spoken by me, before Alex died, and shared with me by others since Alex died. I now tell those others in my newfound wisdom, "There is no off button. You don't die, you just wish you would." Others think of ending the pain through suicide.

This is exactly what I thought I would do if one of my children died. Given my background and who I was at the time, suicide was not an option, but a must. I *must* die because my son is dead. While it did not happen, I lived for a long time thinking that I would soon die.

The path to a form of wellness has been up and down. There have not been any easy answers, but I have learned about *hope*.

I wish to speak to newly bereaved parents who do not think they will live through this nor do they want to. Maybe, just maybe, I can give hope to someone out there who is like I was—living to die and planning to die. I do not feel that way anymore and would like to share the process that brought me to where I am: a still-mourning mother who no longer wishes to die and is constantly finding reasons to live and even occasional joy. There is hope.

I am also writing this book because I wish for the non-bereaved to understand the grief of a mother. The death of a child seems to be a forbidden subject. Conversations stop. People run away or pretend not to see me. This is a sad reflection of our society and its view of death.

Surely, if it were their child who died they would not want people to treat them that way. Understanding very often brings about different behavior and that would be very welcome to *all* bereaved people.

ACKNOWLEDGEMENTS

We have been blessed with many wonderful people in our lives, especially since we started this path of grief. Each knows who they are and have been told of our love for them. For now, from me, thank you for your support and friendship to John, Morgan, and me.

Barb & Leo   You reached out to strangers and became friends in our mutual pain. I will always remember Bradley. (Leo died 2 & ½ years after his son. We still miss him.)

Barb H.   You helped me remember all the important lessons from therapy. You are not afraid to be true and call me on backward movement and encourage me forward. I am glad you are in my life.

Elaine   You know me so well and have been a embodiment of encouragement. I value your friendship and our time spent together.

Jana & Brad	Your kindness and help at The Compassionate Friends is a huge reason I made it. I'll never forget.
Jennie	My friend for thirty-three years and always there when I need to talk. You have nurtured me.
Joyce & Doug	You are both always by our side with your love, support and encouragement. We love you.
Kirsti	Thank you for your guidance with Morgan and your friendship to me. As the bereaved sister of Brad, you understand Morgan's pain and path.
Laurie	My life long friend and bereaved parent of Elizabeth. I am so sorry we both have to do this.
Laurie B	You suffered with me and offered your non-judgmental friendship. I am so grateful.
Marilyn	Bereaved Mom of Chad—thank you for the walks, talks and listening. You are a welcome presence in my life.
Mary	We have become so close and your gentle presence helps my heart.
Mary S.	You nurtured me with massages and let me cry. You heard me. Thank you.
Mike & Val	You saved us on the holidays. We had a home, filled with love, to go to with no expectations put on us.

Sharon	I phoned you for help. You came. I will never forget.
Susan	Together, as bereaved moms, we have struggled on. I reached out to you during one of the worst times. Your friendship means so much to me. I feel as if I know your beloved Drew.
Vicki	You traveled miles to be with and comfort me. You know the pain of losing a brother.
Kelly Osmont	My therapist who allowed me to feel how I felt. I know I was tough, but it is almost five years and I am still here. I didn't believe you. I now do. Thank you

To my sisters, Cindi & Kathy; together we have worked through a lot of pain. I am glad you came back. I love you, both.

There have been others that were part of our lives for awhile. Thank you to our neighbors for bringing in food for a month. Many would arrive at the door and would cry with me. What a gift that was! This was organized by Monica Wright, also a neighbor, who is a very special person. To my book club members, who were a little afraid of my pain, but hung in there anyway. Thank you.

A very special thank you to Dianne Arcangel, whose encouragement was the foundation to start this book. Without her, I don't believe I would have had the courage to actually write it. I am very grateful.

INTRODUCTION

I had been an average person in a happy life and it was very special to me. In a moment's time, my life changed forever. Who I was, died with my son. To stay in this world I had to create a new me. This is the story of how I survived and changed.

"I now experience happiness and joy, but always on top of the perpetual sadness that has become part of my being. This I can live with."

ALEXANDER JAMES HUBER

Long, lean and lanky. These words so describe Alex. I can still see him racing toward me, those long legs loping, without a care in the world. He grins from ear to ear as I say "Slow down, Alex. There's no rush."

"Sure there is," he answers. No real compelling reason, but always rushing through life. Did he know that he had to fit it all into a short seventeen years?

A cascade of fair hair runs down his neck. He wanted to grow it long because he was sure he would go bald like his dad. Maybe length would help slow the inevitable. He wears the ever-present baseball cap, backwards of course, and the hair just peeks out in the back, soft and silky and straight. I loved to tousle it in the morning before he left for school.

Hazel eyes that turn to green more often than not. They sparkle and snap and show his love of life. Gentle features that would make him beautiful if not for the twinkle and ear-splitting grin.

This gentleness and kindness were evident in all he did. Always ready with a willing ear for a troubled friend, even his mom. He understood pain and was prepared with the hug of understanding.

His high school principal, Larry, described Alex as his friend who would listen to his budgetary woes during those times he would drop into the office for a visit.

"How could he have been interested in this?" Larry says.

Yet he offered an ear and a grin of support and understanding, even though he probably didn't understand. "I will miss my young friend. One of the finest young people I have ever known."

Always tucked in his back pocket was a paperback book. He loved to read, inheriting this trait from Mom and Dad. Science fiction and fantasy were his mainstay. He would share these stories with classmates and teachers alike, who couldn't help but be charmed by his infectious smile and enthusiasm: "Alex is happy somewhere in one of his books," said a grieving friend.

Alex loped into the appropriate field of track. He wasn't the fastest, but no one worked harder. Shin splints tortured his legs, but he persisted. Coach described Alex as the heart of the team, always offering encouragement or congratulations for his teammates. He died two days before the first track meet of his junior year. They dedicated it to him and wore black armbands as they ran. The lane he would have been running in opened up during his 100-meter race. He was running with them, certainly.

Lean, lanky Alex could eat like three truck drivers but had a concave stomach. Perhaps after a particularly heavy meal it might pooch a little, but that was the extent of it. Lucky boy could eat forever and stay slim. He was the envy of our household.

If Alex could have had his way he would have lived on pizza. As a matter of fact, he did. The perk of working at a pizza parlor is bringing the mistakes home. Ever generous, he would pack them up the next day and take them to school to share with his friends. I am so pleased for every bite he took that gave him such pleasure.

One of my clearest memories of Alex and our relationship happened during his sophomore year when I picked him up from a school dance one evening. Through the rear view mirror I saw him walking out of school with his arm around the waist of a lovely young lady. She reached up and put her arms around his neck and gave him the sweetest hug. He then sauntered to the car with his face shining with happiness. As he got in and looked at me he saw a huge grin on my face. "Not a word, Mother."

"I'm not saying a word, Alex, but if I were I might ask what it would cost me to find out about this girl."

After much negotiation, at half past eleven, we arrived at the price of two pizzas, deliverable immediately. He then proceeded to spill the story of his love life, including his first kiss. We laughed so hard during this lighthearted conversation and it remains truly one of our finer times together.

Alex died toward the end of his junior year in a car accident.

WAKE UP MY SON

The tears fall silently down my face. Have they stopped even for an instant? I mourn and cry and it seems unending, but how can it end? For I will always cry about my Alex and I will always miss him.

I shiver and cry some more as these thoughts and others run circles through my head looking for resolution. I keen and wail and cry out "How can I live in this world without you?" My child, my child, my tears scream. "How could you die?" No answers, no peace, no time out from grief!

Where were you? You were late and that was not like you. I tried not to panic. The doorbell rang and I shot to it with feelings of unease. My sister, a stranger, and my brother-in-law stood there. "Hi! What's up?" I said. My brother-in-law began to cry and my sister gasped, "Alex is dead. He was in a car wreck."

My blood ran cold and froze in my veins. My body started to shake. I heard in the background my thirteen-year-old son, Morgan, crying "Not Alex, not my brother." The stranger, who was the police chaplain, wrapped me in a blanket to warm the shivering and fight the shock. I knew I had to call my husband, John, who was away on business.

"Honey, honey our Alex is dead." Complete silence as he tried to understand what is not understandable. Maybe when he gets home he can make it all right, I prayed. We picked him up at the airport at three-thirty A.M. but he could not make it all right. Blessedly, my memory of what follows that night and the next day is gone.

My next vivid memory is seeing you laid out in the casket. We went. My poor John collapsed and I, who everyone thought could not endure seeing you, stroked your hair, filled my eyes and soul with your image and begged you to wake up. "Please wake up my son, please open your eyes."

You looked so beautiful, yet so still, as if in a deep sleep. Oh, how I wished. I could have stayed with you forever. My tears had dried for then. The pain was too deep for mere tears to be an outlet. I was frozen in a frigid sea of pain.

"We need music for the funeral."

Music! How can I think about music? I am going to lose my mind. My thoughts immediately went to the song Morgan has been working on. Maybe he could record it. *Somewhere Out There*, he sang to you my son. It was so beautiful, brother to brother. Did you hear?

Six hundred people came and still I was not crying. Did we know this many people? Over three hundred were students. So many stunned eyes and rigid jaws as testament to tears held back. They were being strong for us. When Morgan's song burst forward all the jaws released and the tears flowed. Many spoke of you and what they had loved. I knew you were kind, generous, funny, but I didn't know that everyone else knew, too. Ahhh, true grief for a beloved person, not just my son, but a person who in a short seventeen years had already made a mark in the world.

Pacing around your cemetery plot, crying and wailing and scream-ing, I didn't know how to go on, so I did not. I lived with you at the cemetery for eighteen months. Every day I would bring my chair and sit with you, my baby who was no longer a baby but a man. "How could you be in there and me out here?" This repeated over and over in my head and then I started to cry. All I could do was cry. How could there be so many tears and would they ever stop? Should they stop?

I hear tears are good and create a path toward what the world wants for me—acceptance. Never will I not miss holding you in my arms, or to touch the silkiness of your hair or hear the deep throatiness of your laughter.

One day when I was with a group of people I felt it rising. I didn't know what it was and started to panic. Then it no longer mattered because it was here, the primal scream that ripped through my body and released me from shock. It was the scream and tears that thrust me forward on a path toward acceptance.

My son, my Alex, I will always cry for you, but not at the cemetery very much any more and I will live again, for you and for Morgan and for Dad.

1 A NORMAL TUESDAY

Tuesday, March 15, 1994, a day like any other. I organized my office, paid bills, cleaned house and folded clothes.The addition we had added onto the house for Alex and Morgan had progressed to the last phase and I was also dealing with the contractors about the final touches.This was a huge, beautiful area for the boys to have parties and friends over. Alex's new bedroom and bath were included in the addition so he could have privacy when he started college. After he moved on, it would all belong to Morgan.

I walked around with a feeling of dread all day, almost as if I had to get everything done for some reason. I rushed and felt anxious, but when finished with everything I remember thinking, "Now I'm ready, but for what?" On edge, I decided to run a few errands in town.

On the way down the mountain I had to resist the urge to go by the school and watch Alex drive. "I can't do that when he has given us no reason to suspect him of recklessness," I told myself. While sitting at the stoplight I heard sirens. I quickly checked the time and breathed a sigh of relief knowing my children were still safely in school. Little did I know I was hearing the sirens for Alex's accident. He had died at 2:17 P.M. and I heard the sirens blast at about 2:25 P.M.

I went about my errands. Once at the telephone company, I tripped for no apparent reason. Returning to my car, I couldn't decide where to go or what to do. I still felt out of sorts, as if something were wrong. Finally pulling myself together I went to gather Morgan from school.

Reaching our neighborhood, I noticed a police car at the top of the hill. This seemed very odd for him to be parked there and it made me uneasy. Later I found out that he was watching the house waiting for someone to get home. Why they didn't tell me then remains a mystery.

We went home for about an hour and then it was time to take Morgan to Sylvan Learning Center for his hour lesson. I dropped him off and shopped at Costco for awhile. I bought Alex the video of *The Fugitive* as a surprise.

At ten minutes until six I started calling home from my cell phone to make sure Alex was back from track practice. He was usually home by five thirty. I picked up Morgan and as we headed home I kept redialing. At this point my throat started to tighten in fear and anxiety.

We arrived home and the house felt dark and empty. I rushed to the answering machine looking for a message from him—none. I put my packages down just as the bread machine and the front door bell sounded simultaneously. It was ten past six.

I answered the front door and there stood my sister, a stranger, and my brother in law. I said "Hello. What's up?" My brother-in-law began to cry, which is something I had never before seen. My sister said, "There has been an accident with Alex."

"Where is he? I have to go to him."

"No, Terri. Alex is dead."

My world ended at that moment and for years to come.

Every cell in my body froze. I wanted to run away screaming, but I couldn't move. My body started shaking and I started burning from my throat down to my waist and that burning lasted for four months. The unknown man was the police chaplain and he asked them to get a blanket for me because I was in shock. I fought and wanted to go to Alex, but they wouldn't let me. He had been dead over four hours before I was notified. Why hadn't they let me know sooner so I could be with him?

I must have made some sort of noise because Morgan came out and wanted to know what was wrong. My sister, Kathy, held him by his shoulders while telling him. I vaguely heard his denial through my own shock, "Not Alex, not my brother."

I had to then call my husband, John, long distance and tell him that his firstborn son was dead of a broken neck. He was on a car phone and there was total silence. That silence is etched forever on my brain. That was the silence of shock, disbelief, failure, and despair. In his mind, John felt he had failed to protect his son.

Somehow, he had to manage to get home from Chicago. The kindness of strangers is the only way he did it. His co-worker drove him directly to the airport where he was hand-led to the last flight of the evening to Portland via Las Vegas. He called me from there during the layover, heartbroken, looking at Alex's picture. He was so far away and I felt so helpless.

After I had spoken with John in Chicago, I phoned my friend Sharon. She came immediately to my side and between her and my sister they started to make all the horrible, yet necessary, phone calls. This they did despite their own grief and I will always be grateful.

John's flight arrived at three-thirty AM and the police chaplain drove me to the airport. My first step of looking for the magic wand. I kept thinking, "When John gets home everything will be all right." Of course, it wasn't, but having him home comforted me.

The next day we had to go to the funeral home and make arrangements. I so badly wanted to see him but was physically restrained, for my own good. I suppose I could have fought through, but the weakness of despair left no fight in me. I wish I would have, though, before he had been "fixed up". His skin would have been softer to the touch and, perhaps, a little warmth would have remained. However, we waited until the later in the day.

We didn't have a place to bury him, having never considered the possibility. I wanted him close to home so that I could get to him easily. There is a small Catholic Cemetery nearby and that is where he lay.

We returned home from picking out his burial plot to a house full of people. Having lived in the community for twenty-five years and being active with the schools, we knew a lot of people and had many friends. Nevertheless, it was a surprise to see people whom I hadn't talked with in years. There was a great outpouring of love and we appreciated it.

We went back that evening to the funeral home to see Alex. I was desperate and was sure it was all a mistake, right up until I saw my beautiful son laid out in a casket. He looked like he was sleeping. I kept telling him to open his eyes because he couldn't be dead; it's just not possible. As many parents do I wanted to crawl in with him,. I stroked his hair and spoke his name over and over. John was going through his own version of hell. We were each alone in our own agony as we stood together over our dead child.

There was a viewing on Thursday at the local church, where the service was also held. Hundreds of people came to see Alex, write a message to him on the paper provided, and just cry. So many kids, friends of his; so many adults, friends of ours; teachers and principals from all over the district. This honored Alex so much. The expression of love for him and us was overwhelming.

It would be called a beautiful service, except it that was for my son. There was a lot of love, but he was dead. He was dead. The police chaplain and Minister Rob Blakey opened his church and his heart to us. His words at the service were beautiful and exactly what I wanted. He did not talk about the blessings of Alex in heaven, but about the pain of the survivors and how to continue on with each other, God, and memories.

Morgan had recorded the song *Somewhere Out There* the night before to be played at the funeral. I can't think of anything that Alex would have wanted more. He loved his brother's voice and the words to this song are incredible when sung from brother to brother. John, Morgan and Sharon, and I having declined the privacy of the "relative room" sat in the front pew. I needed to be with the people that loved Alex.

I was told that there were six hundred people at the service but I never turned around and looked. I heard a lot of sobs and knew they loved him, too. We had an open microphone, at which many people, mostly his friends, shared memories, poetry, and their love for him. I listen to the recording of this service every year at the anniversary of his death in an attempt to reconnect with all of that love.

We did go to the graveside in a processional. I don't actually remember very much about it. My mind was so numb with shock that I just wanted everything over so I could spend time with Alex. Except Alex would be buried. I hadn't considered that part.

One of my more vivid memories is very dark. We were being driven home in the funeral limousine and while turning into our neighborhood a cyclist cut off the limo. I was so furious that I wanted to jump out and throttle her. How could she blithely be cycling around and actually hold us up when Alex was dead? Looking back, this is when the dark fury in me started emerging. This woman had no idea what was going on, but to this day I think of her with distaste.

Several friends had arranged a reception at our home. The only thing I know is that I walked in, sat down with my coat on, and did not move again. I don't know who was there or how many or when everyone left. It became silent and we were alone.

So began the rest of my new life without my firstborn son.

As published in Bereavement Magazine, September/October 1997

The Oak Tree
It looks so big, this oak tree.
Sitting, on a slightly slanted hill.
So many branches, so wide, but not perfect;
A lot of bark is missing.

So majestic; minding its own business.
I have wondered if it knows that it
killed my son.
A few feet to either side, he would have
missed hitting it; and dying.

If it could think, what would it think of
all the things written in its flesh.
"He left us too soon," wrote one friend.
"We love you," wrote two others.
Deeply carved letters: Alex Huber
Done by dad—the day after his death.

A large memorial sign—instigated by mom.
Ribbons, flowers, pictures. What would it think?
Would the tree be sorry or would it be
hurting from its own wounds?
Does it notice his mom sitting by it and crying?

I can't hate you tree, you are just a thing. But I
wish you had been somewhere else.

Terri Huber

Dear Alex,

I remember the day you arrived, I didn't scream, I sang through the pain with *Old Macdonald Had a Farm.* I didn't scream when you died, either, I froze in the pain, so much worse than the physical pain of childbirth. I am a really only a shower singer and you, unfortunately, took after me. But we both had a great love of music.

The doctors who performed your circumcision told me it took several nurses to hold your legs down. You were very strong. Maybe I would have fought to. I know there is controversy now about circumcising, but at the time it was the proper thing to do. I hope you forgave us.

We took you home from the hospital in a red velvet poncho. You were so tiny and your little face peeked out at me. Back then we laid babies on their tummies. We got lucky and you did not smother. In fact, when you were about three weeks old I came into your room and found that you had moved all the way to the corner of the crib. I didn't believe it, so I put you in the center again and there you went; this tiny little thing with the strength to scoot at only three weeks old. Little did I know that this was an early indication of hyperactivity.

Before this became an issue we had to get through your colic. The first nine months of your life were extremely difficult. I would feed you, first at my breast and then after six weeks with a bottle, and for the following ninety minutes you would scream in pain. I hurt with you. I also felt as if I would lose my mind from lack of sleep.

Your dad absolutely did his fair share, but he did have to go to work early the next morning. Many a night I would come from our bedroom and find you both asleep in the rocking chair; you lying quietly on his chest. He got up with you, bless his heart. When you weren't crying you were happy and smiling. I felt so sorry for you and me. Finally, you grew out of the colic and your little personality started coming through. Then you started to walk.

You were only nine months old when you took your first steps. Once again, an indication of hyperactivity to come, but to us a small miracle.

You could scoot, crawl, and walk before most babies. You would be exceptional. That much is true, but you were also hyperactive.

It took a long time for me to admit this. I couldn't really leave the house to do the normal things I saw other young moms do, like go to the park, because you would run off. It was impossible to take you to a store or even to a friend's house, unless they were baby-proofed also. My friend Valarie, whom you always called Aunt Val, had Tyler two months after you were born. She also had a two year old, Jason Michael. We about lived at each other's homes, sharing the company and helping out with the kids. Outside of family, she was the first one to the hospital.

Life went along like this until your brother was born. You were immediately taken with Morgan, holding him, helping change his diaper, telling him about your toys. A built-in little friend had been born, but you were so hyper, we were afraid you would accidentally hurt "little brother." You could play a little rough.

About this time someone introduced me to the "Feingold Diet" for hyperactivity. I was skeptical but desperate. You were four years old and we did not know that drugs were available to help. Actually, I am rather glad we didn't, because the diet worked well and that was a better first step.

I remember when we realized the diet was helping you, only four days after you started on it. We took a chance and went to the mall. We'd look at each other and then at you, as you calmly walked along. We didn't chase you once. For the first time ever we had fun with you while shopping. I am so grateful for the Feingold Diet because it gave you your life back.

You were such a happy little boy and I can still see you with your face all scrunched up in a big grin. You had a mischievous twinkle in your eyes and you did lead me on a merry chase. It's funny, but mostly I remember the good times of tickling, reading, watching you, Dad and Morgan building a fort with the sofa pillows. You had so much fun with your Star Wars Action Figures and then on to GI Joes. You could battle with the best and it was so funny to observe. You said you wanted to be a soldier. I don't know if that actually would have worked out because you were so very gentle, but it was a fun dream for you, whatever your idea of soldiering was.

Movies had always been difficult for you to hold still through, but it was getting easier. I did have to sneak your popcorn in, though. You couldn't eat the theatres. I took you to see the *Fox and the Hound* animated movie. You were about six and could easily sit still by that time. This movie had a sad ending and I kept watching you put on a brave little face. While walking out I saw that you were pale and your lips were one thin line. "It is alright to cry, Alex." Your little brow puckered up and you started sobbing. You were so sensitive to the hurt and pain of others', even animated characters. This sensitivity would stay with you the rest of your life.

School! You were so bright and easily adapted to the routine. Studies came easily to you and you became an honor student through sixth grade. You did so well sticking to your food program. You would rattle off the big words of "additives" and "preservatives," which you could not have. You would turn down the candy and cup cakes being passed around in class. The things I had there for you to eat weren't quite the same. I was so very proud of your discipline, while at the same time suffered with you. If we went to an event where treats were being served, I would pass them up along with you and we would have something wonderful later.

There were other difficulties to deal with at school, also. Having been hyperactive at the beginning of your life, you missed learning the social skills that are automatically absorbed. You were so friendly and sweet, but in the world of little boys this was not looked on with much favor. You were constantly teased and often your feelings were hurt, but the worst was yet to come.

One day in fourth grade you came home with some bruises. It took some prodding on my part, but the next thing I knew you were sobbing in my lap. "Four boys held me down during recess, Momma, and they beat on me. My friends only watched. Why didn't they help?" Your little heart was broken and so was mine. I felt so helpless as I held you in your pain. How could these sort of horrible things happen? This event left a permanent scar on your heart, a scar that I carry for you now.

Life continued forward with these occasions becoming more infrequent. You had started to learn the social skills that are so necessary in life. Plus, as you and your classmates got older, your kindness and sensitivity became a welcome commodity. Your peers could and did turn to you for a shoulder to cry on and a sympathetic ear. Had these destructive events happened to you so that you would know about pain and could really be there for them?

I remember your first "date." You asked a girl to the school dance in seventh grade and were sure I would disapprove, so you didn't tell me. Someone else did though and I was able to tease you about it. Your eyes were wide with shock that I could know. You then became sure that I knew all or could find out.

The other thing I remember so vividly is your hate of fruit. Any kind. You didn't mind juices, but the texture of fruit made you gag, especially bananas. You came home from junior high one day and told me about *the race*. It was set up during lunch break and was sort of a relay. At the end of each aisle was a bag with food in it; the person who reached it first had to eat the food before they could continue on. Even though you were a picky eater you saw many kids getting candy and cookies and thought, "Okay, I'll do the relay." Of course, we know what was in your bag: a banana. You were so funny as you told me the story of how hard you tried, really tried to eat this banana. But it wouldn't go down. I'm not surprised. You wouldn't even eat banana anything as a baby or toddler.

High School! The time you had been living for. You had no fear of it and knew it would be your time. You took guitar lessons and even became part of a band. While this didn't have a long life, you had a great deal of fun jammin'.

You started true dating. This was mostly fun to watch, except when you had the broken heart that accompanies girlfriends. You had many friends, both boys and girls, and a very diverse life. We would argue about the hours and phone curfew when counseling a wounded friend.

Mr. Dear Abby of Tualatin High, you took it all to heart. We worried about this but managed to come to terms.

You had many friends from all walks of life. You befriended a boy at lunch who was in a gang. He told me at your funeral that he left the gang because of you. He experienced your acceptance of who he was and cherished your friendship—he was totally devastated when you died, but managed to continue on a good path.

One of my most precious memories is just a moment in time. You, Morgan, and I were walking arm in arm, with me in between you both. At that time you were both taller than I was, but it took awhile for you to get there. This had to be not long before you died. I remember thinking, "This is wonderful. I am between my two sons. They are beautiful and I am happy." I took that moment into my heart and held it close. This was one of the last happy times for many years to come.

Many people cared deeply for you, Alex. They came to your viewing and your funeral in droves. They wrote about their love for you and left mementos of this affection with you. They all suffered and asked the same question, "Why? Why, Alex?" No answers for them or for me. How could someone so kind, gentle, funny, smart and compassionate leave us all behind? Was your work here finished? You certainly had achieved more as a person, through your kindness and compassion, than many adults.

You and I both know part of the reason, though, don't we honey? You were seriously off your Feingold diet the night before your death. While at 17-years-old you didn't stick to it religiously, you did pretty well. I remember, not long before you died, we had a conversation about just this subject. You said, "It's not fair, Mom. Why do I have to be the one affected by these additives? I want to be like everyone else."

I told you that life was not fair and then pointed out others suffering with diabetes, physical disabilities and my own battle with muscular dystrophy. You did understand intellectually but it hurt anyway and I think you rebelled a little. It may be this that cost you your life. If any of us could have realized the horrible possibilities!

You were with two of your closest friends in the car accident. They later told me that your behavior was different on the day of your death. You were rather wound up and since you were a very together young man, usually, this was noticed. You hugged many of your friends at school, earlier in the day, and told them you loved them. Did a part of you know, Alex? These boys were both in comas and were not at your funeral, my son. They suffered terrible trauma and guilt over your death. They miss you, I am sure, as so many do.

You died with the remnant of a black eye given to you by your baby brother. I know it is strange, but it makes me smile. You boys were wrestling around in the hallway of our home. Even though Morgan is three and one-half years younger than you were, he was as tall as you, and a much bigger build. You came out to me with a pained expression and this black eye and I told you, "If you're going to wrestle with a baby grizzly, then you will bear the consequences." You never told anyone how you got the eye because it was embarrassing to let on that your younger brother could best you. But Dad and I sure had fun teasing you about it.

As I write all these things, I go into a place where I still do not believe you are dead. It does not make sense to me, when I look at your picture, that there will be no more. We were becoming even closer as you got older. I told Lennie, your former daycare teacher, that I was sorry she didn't know the young man Alex and about how close we were. She said to me, "Terri, you and Alex were always very close." Those words warmed my heart so much. I had always felt that way, but to know it was obvious validates my thoughts.

I write this book in honor of you, Alex. It is about how to survive when your beloved child dies. I didn't think I would. I didn't want to. I survived anyway. I think you helped me from above.

Thank you for being my son.

Love, Mom

Alexander James Huber January 20, 1977 – March 15, 1994

Picture used with permission from Lifetouch National School Studios

I got out of bed the day after he died. That in itself is a miracle. I got up because I couldn't stand lying there and looking at my husband's half-closed, blood-shot eyes. I couldn't lie there and let my mind free float. I would go crazy. I got up everyday from then on, immediately, when my mind plugged in. I not only got up, but I got dressed and ready for the horrible day to come, even when I was sick.

My first thoughts were always of Alex. The early days it was a searing pain that shot through my head and down to my already burning stomach. "My son is dead. How can I be alive? I don't want to be here." I would look in the mirror as I brushed my teeth, but I couldn't see me anymore. I couldn't make sense of being there and doing something routine like brushing my teeth. Everything seemed so trivial and unimportant. Why should I have to do anything when the pain is overwhelming?

For about the first year, I couldn't tell you what I did during the day. I know I kept my desktop publishing business open, but memories are very vague. I think I must have done what work there was on autopilot. This had been a brand new business and my client list was small. That first year after Alex died I gave it my best shot, but my heart was no longer in entrepreneurship and making money. I closed the business and haven't regretted it. Beyond that, nothing stands out in my memory. We went on the already-planned trip to Hawaii, but I don't remember much about it either. I've heard of this phenomenon from others, so I know it is not unusual to forget that first year and in many ways I am grateful. But it does seem odd that when a memory fragment does come forward, it is very dreamlike. Not very much substance to the first year, only pain, unremitting pain.

The second year I came out of shock. My days still had a surreal feel to them and one just flowed into the next. That feeling left when I was on a weekend retreat with my therapy group.

My counselor was working with someone else when, I felt this odd sensation, as if my head were going to explode. All of a sudden, I heard myself start to scream Alex's name over and over. I couldn't stop for the longest time.

This is the very first time, anywhere, even alone, that I unfroze enough to let the anguish out. I remember trying to scream other times; to beat on pillows with tennis rackets; to break dishes in a safe way. None of this worked for me because it felt artificial. This anguish and release from shock all came out in its own good time and as hard as it was I am grateful it happened. It did not make my pain go away, but it allowed me to start really dealing with what life had given me.

After that weekend, things were not quite such a blur. My life became purely about survival. Before I didn't think I would, could, or should survive and now I was actively looking for a way to do it. Bouts of suicidal depression, however, still plagued me. I stayed in group therapy for another fourteen months, went to Compassionate Friends meetings, participated in a small group of bereaved moms, and read every book I could get my hands on about either grief of a parent or near-death experiences. I didn't feel so alone as I read about the grief of other parents and the books about near-death experiences gave me some comfort that his trip to heaven was wonderful.

All of this was like chasing the magic wand that I could wave and make things better or at least when found it would give me the anwer I was desperate for. Why?

Of course, as I discovered, there is no magic wand. But all the ways I chased it led me to other resources, which usually offered wisdom that would help me through that day. I needed something, anything, that would get me from day to day. This became my mission in life.

Then one day, about three years after Alex died, I ran out of things to do and wands to chase. There were no more news articles to write or pictures and poems to put in the local paper; the first year it had been all right, but now it didn't fit. There would be no more times together at the cemetery for his birthday. My fear was that if I put out the invitation, no one would show. I would have been devastated and couldn't face it. In retrospect, I was wise in this area.

It was also right before this third year anniversary that a catalyst for change came. While at this time I was no longer suicidal, my desire to die was still vibrating. It appeared as if I might get my wish in the guise of breast cancer. While it turned out not to be cancer, I considered letting nature take its course. Should I seek further tests and treatment? I went to the tree where Alex died, cried for the longest time, and realized I had come to a point where I did not want to leave John and Morgan. I didn't know if Morgan could survive losing a mother in addition to a brother and I couldn't conceive of adding more pain to John's life. This is where I came back to life.

I had been running so hard, doing things for and about Alex, that I had not really faced forever. Forever after, on this earth, my son would be gone. I would never hold him again or touch his sweet face. I would not see his children. I would need to find a way to be here, without him, and not continue to feel the hopelessness in this same way. I couldn't face another fifty years feeling like this.

My path once again changed to continuing to deal with grief, but also looking for a way to come back into life. My way! It would be different than others, because I am me. A portion of my life would always be dedicated to Alex and his memory, but it was time for me to become the person I would want him to be proud of. When I see him, I would like to hear the words: "You did good, Ma. You fulfilled your destiny." I am trying, Alex, everyday.

3 A PART OF MY HEART

Christmas 1993! Three and one-half months until Alex would die. Of course, we did not know this and went about Christmas as any other, or almost. We had too much work, too little time, and spent too much money. Sounds pretty normal for this time of year. We did do one thing differently though, we video-taped our Christmas morning. Ostensibly, we did this to send to John's parents, but since we had been apart from them at Christmas for twenty-three years and had a camcorder for ten, I now wonder at the reasons. I am so happy to have this recording, which I watch every Christmas.

Shortly before this holiday, Alex asked if he could have a car for his gift. Of course, this was mostly tongue-in-cheek because he knew we would not get his 16-year-old self, who did not even have a driver's license yet, a car. But it became a running joke between he and I.

One day I was at a local craft fair and ran across an ornament I thought would be perfect. It was a dough art boy with blond hair, sitting in a car. On the rearview mirror were attached miniature dice and along the front was written "First Car." I decided to get this for his stocking.

I'll never forget his face when he pulled this out. He got the joke immediately. "Very funny, Ma!" He laughed all day and we had so much fun with it. Alex never put the ornament on the tree. He kept it on his desk. I didn't actually realize this until after he died.

A day before his funeral I was in his room. My mind kept thinking, "He will be so lonely without his things." He kept all the letters, cards, and notes in a desk drawer, for several years. I pulled all of these out, went through them, and decided they must go with him. I have lived to regret this impulsiveness. We decided his phone and answering machine must be with him also. They were the staples of his social life. I was at last sitting still at his desk when I saw the ornament. I know I don't have to tell the bereaved parent reading this what it felt like. I knew it had to be with him.

I went to the viewing area at the church and put all of this in with him. As I went to lay the ornament by his hand, the dice fell off. I put them back on; I took them back off; I went through this several times and finally decided to keep them. This, I do not regret. They have given me comfort.

These mini dice are only hot glued together and I was so afraid of losing them that I had a pendant made to protect them. I had asked the jeweler for a teardrop, but it came out differently. I don't know if they could not make a teardrop or what, but this is really better. It is a round gold band, one-quarter inch deep and has glass on either side. The dice are suspended in the middle by their pink ribbon. The jeweler thought the rattle might be some comfort and did not anchor it. He was right.

I wear this pendant on a forty-inch chain, always. It rattles when I walk and I think of it as a whisper from my son. "Keep going Mom. You can do it!" I am far too attached to it and would be devastated if anything happened, but that is how it is. I hold onto it during times of anguish and stress. It is neither my good luck charm nor a pretty piece of jewelry, but a part of my heart.

For a long time I wore this outside my clothing for the world to see and hoping they would ask. Some would shudder and turn away as they heard what they meant; others would say how wonderful they thought it was. Eventually, it was no longer important that others ask and now, much of the time, I wear it under my clothing. It hangs warm against my skin and I know it is there. That is all that really matters.

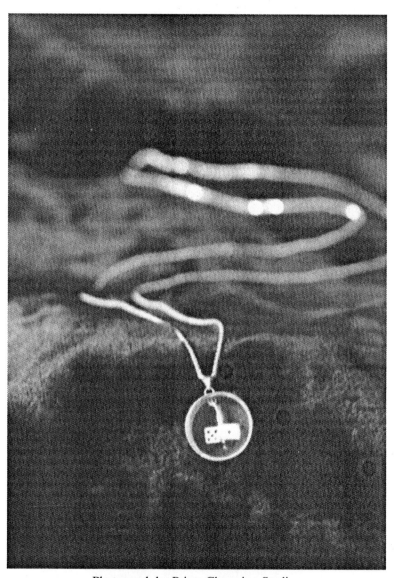

Photograph by Prints Charming Studios

Green Eyes Smiling

Green Eyes smiling in my mind,
It's only happiness frozen in time,
From little rascal
Into handsome young man
Nothing held you back or down
You were always smiling,
You had no time for frowns.

Just like a flower
We watched you bloom,
From sweet baby face
To rugged jaw dude
Black back hat to cover your head
Long lean and lanky, toes to head.

Special were your assets,
Touching hearts so many
A rich young man you were
And not in the way of pennies.

Friends, you had so many
From many different stations
Some you knew who had no cares
Others dealing with life's many fears

Always there to lend an ear (or hand),
Always there to help
Sometimes when helping others
You forgot about yourself.

What made you who you are, the driving force?
That made you a shining star?

For you could always see some good,
Even when you understood
But you could see beyond.

Spring is here, the sun, the sky,
Cause me to reflect and
To wonder why
I see no rhyme or reason
I couldn't see a sign
But now I close my eyes and keep seein'
Your green eyes smiling on my mind.

J. P. Huber • March 1994

4 SIX MONTHS AND HE IS STILL GONE

September, the beginning of the school year. Morgan would start eighth grade, but Alex would not start his senior year. This is just not possible. I wanted him to be a senior and to experience the prom; to have a portfolio of pictures done; to participate in the senior prank; and mostly, to walk at graduation with his friends. He has to be here. He isn't.

My mind could not accept the horror of this. It was at this time that I was most vulnerable to suicide. I needed to see him so badly, to ruffle his silky hair and have him give me a big bear hug and kiss me on the tip of the nose. My arms would reach out into thin air to try to find him, but they wrapped only around myself. Holding my arms tight around me, I rocked back and forth. The pain was so intense, even worse than in the beginning. The reality was sinking deeper into my being as some of the shock wore off. My mind would snap around looking for some relief, but none was to be found.

Usually during times like these, I'd find myself at the cemetery cutting a path in circles around his grave. Pacing and crying, pulling at my hair…how could my son be in this hole in the ground. Reaching down I would pull at one of the squares of grass that covered him up.

Somewhere in me I could envision myself digging, but managed to find restraint. After all, what good would it do.

Then, lying down on top of the grave I wished to die. Feeling the cool grass on my cheek I could imagine myself just sinking into the ground. While lying on my son's grave, I was teetering on the edge of sanity.

I will always believe that Alex helped me through those moments, sending strength and love and images of Morgan. I had to stay here for Mo. Killing myself, would tell him, "Alex is more important than you are." This could not be further from the truth, but the pain and despair only allowed me to see who was missing from my life. It took a long time for my focus to shift. Somehow, I got through that six-month period and was able to breathe for a bit.

During this time, it appeared as if the world was forgetting Alex. I was so angry about this and about the careless things people said to me. I needed to get these feelings out and so began my first attempts at writing.

Outside of a letter, I had never written anything before. However, I was compelled by some inner knowledge that I needed to do more than journal. My pain had to be witnessed. It was so big that I felt as if I would explode if the world didn't know this wonderful young man had died and how painful it was for me. Our local paper has a column that anyone can write a piece for. I wrote this first article with anger in my heart, and, for me, this was very powerful. I put my frustration out in the world and was able to let the biggest part of that same frustration go.

Having spoken my peace, the world now knew that I thought a lot of them did not have a clue about the pain of grief and loss. I didn't need to dwell on it anymore.

I have since realized that I needed to focus my attention anywhere but on Alex's death. I became extremely incensed by the behavior of others, but now know my reaction was disproportionate. The remarks and small cruelties are not right by any means, but they really aren't even in the same universe as what I have suffered from Alex's absence.

My mind needed the break and went towards the obvious anger that I was carrying anyway; an hysterical anger that went to the core of my being. Tryng to make sense of my child's premature death was something I had to accept—but it seemed impossible at the time. However, taking it out on other people, because they can't know my grief, was not productive. It held me in the place of despair and anger. There really is not a way for them to truly understand the devastation to my life when my son died. I have accepted that for the most part the non-bereaved will never really know what it is like…nor do they want to. I appreciate the people who try, though, because of their love for me and in memory of Alex.

As published in the Tigard Times on September 22, 1994
There is No Vacation From Grief
On March 15, 1994 our 17-year-old son, Alex Huber, was killed in an auto accident. I am not writing specifically about that, but the aftermath. I have discovered, in talking with other bereaved parents at Compassionate Friends, a support group for bereaved parents, that the aftermath is not unique to our family: the pain of seeing an empty room every morning, the knowing he won't be around at the end of the day, his singing, his humor—the grief goes beyond unbearable. But the way some friends and family react is a different pain and very puzzling. It's as if we have done something wrong—because our son died. We know it is not intended to be hurtful, but people aren't aware how painful it is.

Two months after Alex died some people put a great big grin on their otherwise pale faces and tried to pretend that nothing had happened to us. They asked if we weren't just having a wonderful summer. One woman asked our 14-year-old son, who is big for his age, when he was going to start driving, and she was actually urging him on. This person knew Alex was driving when he died.

We've received many comments, undoubtedly with the best of intentions. But they cause pain instead of the intended comfort. Here are a few:

•The people you happen to run into who say, "I just can't handle it, so I haven't called you". (Isn't it a shame they can't handle it? Sure wish we could walk away and not deal with it.)

•"Rejoice, he's with God." (Knowing he is with God does not help the pain of him not being with us. After all, God gave us the nurturing instinct.)

•"God took your child for his reasons. You just need to put it in his hands." (People saying, God did this to you are being the most cruel. Regardless of religious belief that statement only causes pain.)

•"The time for grieving is over and you need to get on with you life."

•"I haven't called because I didn't want to cry in front of you." (Crying and mourning for someone's dead child is a gift to them. It shows how much you care.)

•"I didn't know what to say." ("I'm sorry" or "What can I do".)

Then there are the silent ones, the "friends"—good friends that you never hear from again. They appear for the funeral and say all the right things, but you never get a phone call or visit again. Close friends, that could hold you and help with their mere presence, turn away. Other friends you run into who say, "I will call you soon" and then never do. Perhaps their calling would have been the one bright spot in the day, if they had. Some people think they are sparing you pain by not mentioning your child again. They aren't. Hearing his name is the greatest gift of all.

Exactly how long does it take to "get over" the death of a child? After six months people no longer want us to be sad over the loss. Our child was with us for 17 years. Are we supposed to forget him or no longer miss him after only six months? My heart hurts so bad all the time and the pictures of his maimed body are with me always. There are times, when I see some people and can tell they are thinking; "I would be doing better than this, if it were my child." How can they know? Until you have lost a child you can't fathom the guilt, anguish, never-ending agony of mind and heart. There is no vacation or time out from grief. Instead of the silence, instead of the judgment, it would be much better to just say, "I'm sorry that it is still so hard," and let it go at that. Just showing that you care and not judging are more help than anything.

People have said, "Why don't you call me?" As with many bereaved parents, I do not have the strength to make phone calls. I don't know what to ask for except my son and no one can help with that. Maybe they don't realize how much easier it is if they call me.

We are blessed with many friends who have been a great comfort and support to us. Some of their words have been consoling. But other words have been a torment. Many bereaved parents have suffered through most of these good intentioned hurts. My wish is that people would just think first. All bereaved parents really need to hear is, "I'm sorry and I miss him too."

Restless Nights

Night falls,
And the Dreams begin,
Can one ever win?

Do I sleep,
Or really weep?
Why the day so quickly?

Sorrow races over my brow,
Time etches only new shadows
A smile or soft grimace?

DreamMaster, let me wake!
Let the fantasy be through
Let me be done with you!

Dreamscape beckons,
Draws me on
Can this futile race be won?

Where is night's end
Does new reality begin?
Climb another virtual mountain.

Gather strength,
Make the charge
One more empty summit.

Strength is ebbed,
Where is dawn's light?
Can I survive another night?

A new day dawns
I've had no rest
Oh DreamMaster, you've won your jest!

Hazy day, again,
Stretches before me
I only wish that I could see.

J.P. Huber · 4/94

5 ANGRY AND DIDN'T KNOW IT

I'm sure it sounds odd that a person can be angry and not realize it, but it was true for me as well as many other bereaved parents.

Alex died in a car crash in which he was the driver, with his license of only three months. He was going forty-five miles per hour in a designated twenty-five miles per hour, on gravel. He tried to slow down but his lack of experience cost him his life. Alex did not know to not hit the brake on gravel, but to lift his foot off the accelerator. Having this knowledge could have saved his life.

He lost control of the car and it skid about two hundred feet into a huge oak tree, around which his side door wrapped. Alex died instantly from a broken neck. His friend on the passenger side flew through the front windshield and suffered grave injuries. His friend in the back was injured but did not lose consciousness. When rescue workers arrived he was screaming Alex's name and for help.

Being angry with Alex was something I unable to do. After all, I loved him and felt that somehow this was my fault. I didn't teach him well enough or say the right things for him to understand the consequences of dangerous driving. The driving school didn't teach him well enough. I should have picked a different one. He was only seventeen-years-old and didn't know better. I had this all rumbling around in my mind. Since I couldn't blame Alex and had no one else to blame, I stormed around with what has been described to me as "sparks of anger" screaming from my body. Obviously there was no one to be angry with so I would tell people I wasn't.

This was first brought to my attention about seven months after Alex died. John and I had been participating in a grief project facilitated by a local hospital. At the end of the ten-week period, the facilitator addressed each participant and emphasized their coping strengths and areas of concern. Then she came to me. Mostly, there were a lot of positive things. After all, since the death of Alex it was a positive that I was breathing. She ended with, "You should look into addressing your anger." Me? Angry! I was shocked and had thought I was handling things great. My humor had returned, granted with a very sharp edge. The people who walked away from me, not important, may they experience life altering pain. I still didn't see these as anger issues about Alex's death, but as just and right because people were fools to not understand how hard it is to lose a child. The chip I carried on my should was huge. I hated the world because it carried on when my precious son had died.

I respected this woman's opinion not only because she was a grief therapist but was also a bereaved mother, so I did listen to her assessment. She referred me to a local grief therapist, who had also lost a child to death. Over the next eighteen months I discovered how very angry I was, with Alex, with the world, with myself. I only realized it as it dissipated from my body. The release of that anger is one of the kindest things I have ever done for myself. It had kept me locked up, in despair and hopelessness with no thought of a future. Only after it lifted was I able to see a ray of light, to believe in hope.

The biggest portions of this anger and despair have left me. There are tendrils, however, that occasionally try to take me back into the black hole. I have tools now to fight them off and I use them. I learned how to separate grief from destruction and how to feel love and joy without guilt. "Stay in the moment" became my mantra for survival. This may be a battle for the rest of my life, but I will stave it off as I continue learning how to live with the constant pain of grief.

Missing You

Time will heal all wounds,
They say!
Yet, time moves oh so slow today
And life's tether has slackened
Its pull.

To tarry me here in grief and sorrow,
I worry not yet, about tomorrow.
The sun to rise,
And sleep to wane
As I suffer through the pain.

Oh, young prince you left untimely,
Why the hurry to knock on journey's door?
Our love for you was not used up,
Look! See! I can give another cup!
Too late, you've already journeyed on.

I see a smile through sunlight's shadow,
I recognize that happy fellow.
Too brief, the glimpse
I thought I knew,
Softly, footsteps echo through

I cannot follow, if it's you,
You see, my work is not yet through,
Yet, watch over your brother, mother and me,
And soon, before eternity,
We'll join with you again in family unity

J. P. Huber · 3/94

6
TO THERAPY OR NOT

What can I do? Could a therapist help at all? They can't bring Alex back, so what good would it do. Yet, what do I have to lose? This agony of pain is driving me to self-destruction. I cannot self-destruct though, because of John and Morgan. How could I cause them more pain, but how can I live with this pain? My friend finds a therapist for me.

Sue is a grief counselor. I go to her office and cry; she holds me and I cry. She hears me and for the moment and that is all I need. I live for the weekly visit where I can let go all the tears without considering the feelings of others.

I see Sue for about six months and there doesn't seem to be any place else to go with it. I still cry, but as I had thought before there really isn't much help. She can't bring Alex back and anything short of that isn't enough. I quit seeing Sue.

Around Alex's eighteenth birthday, nine months after his death, I knew I was in deep trouble. All I could think about was dying. All I wanted was to be with Alex. Two times I decided to end my life, but as I went to do this, visions of Morgan flashed through my head. I could not do this to him. How could I live with this pain?

For the longest time I wore only dark clothes; I quit wearing make up and taking care of my physical appearance. After all, I could no longer see myself in the mirror and didn't even bother to look anymore. I could not focus on my reflection and what did it matter anyway.

For many years, I had struggled to keep my weight balanced but would have been happy to lose some. A few months after Alex died I realized my weight was drastically falling off. Immediately, I panicked and thought, "There will be no benefit from my son's death." This was the beginning of a serious weight gain. I didn't care. My son was dead and my life didn't matter. Besides, I was only waiting to kill myself. At that time, what I was waiting for wasn't clear, but I truly believed I would know when the time was right or I would be overwhelmed and just do it.

Through a referral I found a psychotherapist who specialized in grief counseling, Kelly Osmont. I finally realized that if counseling were going to help, I would have to see a person who also lost a child. In my mind, she was the only person who could truly understand. Kelly's empathy, experience and expertise were exactly what I needed. This was the first step toward trying to actually live life without Alex.

Kelly is a small lady with a kind smile who had lost her son about fourteen years earlier. This was a place to start. She had lived through this. How? All I wanted to do is die. That day she was able to exact a promise from me that I would live for five years: "I promise I will not take my life." She promised that at five years, life and the raw pain of grief would be better.

This path through therapy was not easy. It took a long time for me to understand that I was separate from Alex and my life mattered. I was a super-mom. My children would have the kind of life, love, and protection that I never had. The connection to them was so deep and hands on, that I believed I had to die because I had failed to protect one of them. Even though Alex was a young adult and made his fatal choice, I was drowning in a sea of guilt. People told me it wasn't my fault, but this was a realization I had to come and know on my own. I had a lot of baggage that I brought with me into grief and this contributed to my self-destructiveness, with Alex's death being the last straw. I finally released the guilt but it was a process, not a sudden revelation. This is how therapy helped me. The process helped me understand the depth of my despair and some of the reasons for it, which opened my heart to hope.

This was one gift that my precious son left behind—I had no choice but to try to fix me. However, I would most certainly have returned to being who I was to have my son back. The trade-off was not even. But nobody offered that option, and I could not live with the pain the way it was. I was in private and group therapy for eighteen months. This step was the biggest reason I am still alive. As I write this, it has been four years since Alex left this world and Kelly was right; it is better, much better.

Remembering Alex

Fading Laughter
Fleeting shadows across my mind
Colored glimpses of the past
Green eyes that twinkle
Lean blue jeans
Black Back hat, always on the head
Fine brown locks, hidden from my view
Now that you're gone
What are we to do?

You were just taking wing
And though still on a string
You took responsibility
Perhaps with too little care
You didn't know, and didn't realize
The consequences that were waiting there.

Now life's objects have no clarity
Knowing only grief to feed despair
As I lift my eyes

To see dull, gray skies and wonder,
How can this be so?
Why did our Alex have to go?

You lived in such a hurry
Your life a frenzied rush
As if you always were aware
That 17 years, my son
Were all that you could spare.

Now constant pain and grief
Mask our love and joy,
While warm memories still linger
You see that's all we've left,
Since you're gone, my boy.

Slowly, time moves ever onward
Like the drifting of warm sand,
But in a life like this,
How do we find some joy?
That's so hard to understand
Since we've lost our boy.

How do we find new happiness?
Learning what normal now must be.
Just a short time ago
We were a happy Four
But now we live,
, As a sad and lonely three.

J. P. Huber · 5/94

7
THE COMPASSIONATE FRIENDS

Where could I go? There must be a place for me to get help. Somehow a newsletter for The Compassionate Friends got to me. There is a group for people who have a child die? I have to go…they can make it better. This was the beginning of my chasing the magic wand of making it better.

After Alex had been gone for only three weeks, I found myself at a meeting, along with my husband, John. I went to this meeting as if it were my lifeline to sanity. The first thing that took me by surprise was to hear people laughing. How could they laugh? My son is dead. Then I remembered that they too had a child die. One day I would come to understand and occasionally join in with this laughter. Unbelievable!

We found a place in the circle of chairs and took turns telling our story. I couldn't believe all the pain…all the ways to die…all the suffering. It was horrible, but I didn't feel so alone anymore. Other people were hurting like we were. I wasn't singled out, into this madness, by the powers that be.

When it was my turn to speak, I remember being unable to do so, but John did. His voice thick and so close to tears, he spoke about our boy. I was too terrified to actually utter the words "Alex is dead." That would have made it too real.

This was the beginning of a path that took me to three different Compassionate Friends meetings every month for the next six months. I lived for those meeting, where I was able to talk about Alex and my pain. I sat there in my own fog of anger, pain, and disbelief, but it was all right. These people knew and understood and let me be how I needed to be. I could cry, express anger and disbelief all at the same time and they didn't question why. I was offered affection and understanding. Never did I feel judged because I wasn't moving forward on an artificial time line.

For me, the best part of these meeting was sharing my son and getting to know the other children who were lost to their parents. This sharing of pain and the support I received from other grieving parents was a huge step towards being able to manage my heart-wrenching grief. John felt these meetings were not for him and only attended the Christmas memorials. He felt the raw grief to be more overwhelming than helpful.

About eighteen months after Alex's death, I took on the responsibility of editing the newsletter for my local T.C.F. chapter. As a desktop publisher, the layout and design proved not to be a problem, but I had not actually considered the emotional involvement. Because I cried so much, the first newsletter took about twenty-five hours. As time moved on the hours decreased. Eventually I could produce the newsletter in about twelve hours. I would look for articles and allow extra time for emotions. Once at the computer, though, I was able to become somewhat dispassionate, because I had already cried the tears over these heartbreaking pieces. Doing this allowed me to express my grief through creativity. Trying to find the right articles and poems for others helped my own grief in a positive way.

The only downside I found was that the newsletter editor position elevated me to the chapter steering committee. I was so newly bereaved that I was still at the point where the day-to-day business of running the chapter seemed so cold. Plus, despite what we represented, people would be people and politics did come visiting. I believe that I became involved too soon after Alex's death. Even though a mostly positive experience, I would have benefited more by waiting awhile longer.

After one year, I left this position and moved on to a smaller chapter, where I did a simpler newsletter and worked with far fewer people. I functioned better in this environment.

Gradually, I came to a place where I only needed to attend one meeting a month. To this day I can hardly believe that I, a person who hated emotionally charged group situations, could gain so much in the way of trust, compassion, and acceptance. I am grateful to all of my compassionate friends, many of whom have become very close personal friends, as well.

After almost five years, of involvement, I have resolved much. The theory says that to reach a place of acceptance we must tell our story one-hundred times. I spoke of the accident at least this much and no longer feel the continual need to talk about the tragedy that overwhelmed my existance, but I still do and will always talk about my wonderful son. I have become inactive with The Compassionate Friends, having received help, giving back and now moving on to other things. I firmly believe that there is a right time for everyone to leave and that they will know in their hearts when that is. If, down the line, I have a desire to be with other bereaved parents, it is a comfort to know they will be there.

It Is Time

I'm leaving.
Progress they say
And healing.

It is time.
It feels right, but
I am sad anyway.

Once again, change.
Always fluctuating,
this life.

I need change to grow,
which I must do, but
it is unsettling.

My son died and left me.
Change!
I had to then.
Only unthinkable trauma that time.
How to survive?
I still miss him so.

I now leave the life-saving companions
who helped bring me to this point.
It is a positive movement that is welcome,
though a little frightening.

I must approach the world again,
without the cushion.

Am I ready?
I think so, I want to be.
I know so!
Thank you my compassionate friends.

Terri Huber, Alex's mom
Washington County TCF, OR

When Time Stands Still

When time stands still
I'll be with you again
No cares or fears,
I'll be with you again.

When time stands still
I'll feel the thrill again
I'll hold you near
and never cry again.

Time has robbed my heart
My hopes, my dreams
Were torn apart.
The only thing that's real,
Is knowing when time stands still
I'll begin to feel, again.

When time stands still
My love can grow again
My heart can be free with love
To awake and to beat again.

When time stands still
You will be waiting there,
Your smile again, to share.
But only when,
Time stands still.

J. P. Huber · 1/12/95

8 *PEOPLE COMING—PEOPLE GOING*

I suppose I should have realized that it would also happen to us. I had heard at Compassionate Friends and read in different books that when a child dies, friends leave their lives in droves. Many different reasons are given from "They think it is catchy" to "They don't know what to say."

For the longest time, I was in such a fog of shock, I didn't notice the absence of some of these people. About four months after Alex died, it dawned on me that I hadn't seen or heard from several people since the day of the funeral. These were friends that had been a daily part of my life, including someone who referred to me as her best friend. My grief reaction to Alex's death left me unable to pursue any-body for answers. I couldn't even pick up the phone and dial a num-ber. It seemed impossible.

I was too numb with shock about Alex's death to devote much time to worrying about this, but I was puzzled. I became angry! My son had died. How could they do this to me? Didn't they care? But I was in such a world of dysfunction that handling it was beyond my ability. One friend waited a year before she left. Was I so hard to be around or had they set a timetable on my grief? I'll never know. Eventually I let all of them go in both my mind and heart.

I have found in this long walk through grief that some positive always exists to counter-balance the negative. For every person that left my life, two others showed up. With some we had only been acquainted through school activities, but they were touched by the death of this young man and wanted to help and be of comfort. They called, came by, dropped cards of encouragement, and most importantly, let me cry and mourn in their presence. These people have become truly the best of friends. I never have to question their support for me or mine for them.

An interesting thing has happened, though. I don't miss the ones that left, nor do I hate them. I wouldn't want them in my life, however, because I now know the fair-weather friends that they were. I am a different person than I was before, and I need to be true to myself. I can't pretend to not grieve anymore, just to keep a friend or avoid making someone uncomfortable. What I have found is a deepening relationship with the people that stayed.

When I need to, I can talk with them about Alex and how I am feeling, but many times now we talk of other things. I have also realized a depth of caring for other people in myself that I hadn't been aware of before, or maybe it just wasn't there. I don't remember. Now I am able to give them active support through life's twists and turns, even as I continue mourning.

At this point in my life, I can actually thank the people who left my life for leaving. I needed to be taken care of for a long period of time and their fear of witnessing my pain and phobia of thinking Alex's death was catchy, would have made it impossible for me. I know they suffer guilt for having turned away. I hope they never experience the loss of a child. Only then would they really know how they made me feel; abandoned and lonely in a world of intact families.

In the meantime, I am grateful for the blessings of many new friends and the continued love of old friends. While I didn't realize it at the time, they helped me find and hang onto that thread of hope. If they cared so much, maybe my life did have some value. How could I have done this without them?

Dark Side of the Moon

An empty heart since love has gone.
With you gone, why go on.
All my days are cold and lonely
Colorless days with darkened haze.

Living like this is just like dying
I need a place to hide
Where everyday's the same
Only the night eyes of the universe can see

You see there ain't no sunshine
My heart's a barren waste
Yet I can't make a new beginning
If I need a place to hide my fears
A place where I can bury my tears.

I want no one to see me
No one to hear me cry
'Cause they can't feel my pain
And since you're gone
I just as soon
Be living on,
The Dark Side of the Moon.

J.P. Huber · 7/6/94

As published in the Oregonian, March 13, 1995

Her Child's Death Also Killed the Old Terri

I get up everyday, thinking "How can I do this another day"? The waves of depression and despair rush over me for the umpteenth time since he died. Ten months and the world expects me to be "normal". How can I ever meet that expectation of normal again after the death of my child? There is a whole silent underground of us grieving parents. I put on this face, as they do, and continue on...when my heart continues to break.

Would anything really help? Not really, but...perhaps it is made more difficult when someone says "Haven't you moved on yet?" or a similar statement always directed at "getting over it." Sometimes they just stay away, so in addition to dealing with grief, I have to build a new life.

Unless someone has specifically lost a child he does not know how I feel and cannot. I do understand they want the old Terri back, but the horror of my child dying before me has eliminated the old me. I am slowly rebuilding a new me.

Since Alex's death I have seen the very best of people and the very worst. I have seen kind neighbors bring food and offer consolation. I have seen acquaintances reach out constantly and become good friends. I have seen good friends offer their hands and hearts in support in every way possible. I have seen teachers and school staff bend over backward to help us and our other son.

Unfortunately, I have also seen people behave in a manner that I am sure they are not proud of. I have had my family turn away, for no apparent reason—they just do not call or come around.

This has also been the pattern with a couple of good friends. I have not seen them since the funeral. I do know that this behavior is not unique in regard to bereaved parents.

I wish people understood not only what they do to me, and others, but what they do to themselves. I would not want to be them and bear the guilt of having turned away from someone in need who they had cared about.

Yet, it is so hard to be me, because that person is being redefined as a mother who must live in this world without one of her children. My child has died and his death has robbed me of my life…for now.

Despite what some people may think, I really am trying to move forward. But that does not mean not grieving him or forgetting him or crying for him. It means continuing to get up every day and face "it", and the world, and trying.

9 *THOSE SPECIAL DAYS I DREADED*

They loomed ahead of me like black clouds of doom. I remember thinking about Christmas just a few weeks after Alex died and it was only April. How would it be possible to celebrate the holidays without him? Surely they wouldn't show up! I couldn't begin to imagine it and the fear in me was palpable. It felt as if the world were going to make me have Thanksgiving and Christmas. Even worse, Alex's eighteenth birthday would closely follow on January twentieth. Before all of that, however, was the previously-planned trip to Hawaii in August.

When all these thoughts entered my head, I just wanted to give up. During these early days I thought constantly about ending my life. It seemed too much to bear to not only have my son die, but then to have to participate in all the upcoming special days. It would have been so easy to take my life, but being so dysfunctional, I didn't plan ahead on how to accomplish this deed and during the attacks of despair, which were so heinous, many times I was unable to move. Lethargy may have saved my life.

We had been planning the trip to Hawaii for about a year, intending to take the boys on what may have been the last full-family vacation. Alex was on a path to college and we just weren't sure whether he would be around in summers to come. (It seems so ironic now.) So, things were all set and then our boy died. I wanted desperately to cancel this unimaginable vacation, but Morgan looked at us and said "Won't you take me to Hawaii?" It sounded as if he didn't think that he was reason enough to go. Somehow we instinctively knew we needed to do this for him, so he would really know that we loved him as much as we loved Alex. We were a very sad-looking, non-functioning threesome on the beautiful island of Kauai. I personally do not recall very much about this trip.

The three of us spent our first Thanksgiving alone. We had some dinner and then spent the day at the theatre. Movies seemed a great escape and a good way to just get through that painful day.

Our first Christmas we left town and went to be with some good friends. They lived a distance from their families and would also be alone at the holiday season. Our boys had been raised together so it was like being with family. They had no expectations about how we should be and that was a great relief. It was so different to be away from my own home at Christmas that I could almost convince myself that it wasn't Christmas. They did things very differently, thank goodness, so I did not have to deal with rituals that seemed empty with my Alex gone.

At home, we did have an artificial Christmas tree, which we set up right before we left. In Oregon, it is almost sacrilege to go artificial with the beautiful abundance of trees in our area, but we couldn't face getting a real tree as we traditionally had. Going without a tree wasn't an option, because of our younger son. He just looked at us with sad eyes and we knew we had to create some semblance of a holiday for him. Decorating that first Christmas tree without Alex, was one of the more difficult things that I have done.

The day I feared the most, but also had the most control of, was Alex's birthday. I was terrified of facing January 20th with him in the grave, but I could make the day be about him. When I dedicated time to a remembrance of him, it was the closest I had come to being happy since he died. I put an announcement in the local newspaper, which said that there would be a gathering of Alex's friends and family at the cemetery to honor his eighteenth birthday.

The day arrived bright and sunny in the middle of winter. I bought bouquets of balloons and felt markers for people to write messages. I also set up a table with photo albums and Alex's favorite dessert, brownies. People started arriving and I was overwhelmed and touched by the turnout. Of course, his close friends and ours were there. His school principal came and others who wanted to just honor him.

For the most part, we shared memories and our sadness. Then we each took a balloon and wrote a message to him and simultaneously released them. The sky was awash with color and, even though it doesn't make sense to me, I felt better. I still find that sometimes an activity such as this makes me feel better, yet don't understand why. I have learned to just accept it and do what I need to remember my son.

The next event to be faced was Alex's high school graduation, which would include an awards ceremony. There had been a lot of money donated to the "Alex Huber Memorial Scholarship Fund" and I was asked to give a speech and award this to the recipient. Although I had also been involved in the process of determining who would receive this scholarship, when I was first asked my initial reaction was "No!" I would never be able to maintain my composure, while standing before hundreds of people. After some thought and a couple of weeks, I changed my mind. I realized that this would be the very last time that anything would revolve around or involve Alex. I could use this opportunity to speak his name, share his personality, and honor him in a way that no one else could.

Excerpts from my speech given at the awards ceremony in June 1994:

The last two years of Alex's school life were some of his happiest. He loved Tualatin High and felt a strong bond with his classmates and his teachers. I think this speaks highly of them. Alex did not give his friendship lightly and therefore the people he cared about must be special.

This scholarship was set up by classmates who raised funds and by private donation from the many people who care about Alex. The criteria were sent to teachers who then submitted names of students who have attributes similar to those of Alex. While each person is unique, all the nominees portrayed the same friendliness, warmth and likability of Alex. This was especially true in the chosen student.

I would like to read the words that came to me while contemplating this occasion. Words that Alex would speak if he were able.

I am your friend

You are mine

Please remember me in music
and in
Laughter

I am still singing
and
I know all the words.

John accompanied me on stage and handed the certificate and check to Kelly, Alex's friend. I truly feel that I was guided by Alex, because the words felt so right. Kelly had shared a story about Alex "knowing all the words to all the songs" when they had driven around together. I have never written anything poetic in my life, yet these words came into my head as I was trying to sleep. I know they came from my son as a gift for his friend.

The audience did witness my tears and the occasional crack in my voice, but I feel fine with that. Alex not being in this world requires tears and mourning, and as long as I could carry on I didn't mind them knowing that I continue to cry for my son.

Carrying through with this speech is one of the factors that helped me realize my need, ability, and desire to speak out. My forum came in the manner of reaching out to high schoolers in an effort to save their lives.

Fear of the unknown, the ache of debilitating grief, and the desire to be with my son made each day almost impossible and during the first year, those special days were the hardest. What I learned, though, is that I did survive those times and that I must have a plan to get through the many more that would arrive in life, my life, no longer Alex's. His birthday, Christmas, Thanksgiving and others have never become easy, and granted, some are rougher than others, but I have gradually found my pace and do not live in a place of dread so much anymore.

The big key for me was learning and living the four words "stay in the moment." I had to learn that the intensity of pain could not maintain itself and that if I could stay in that moment and not project that I would always feel like this, then it would pass by before too long. Once these moments of agony passed, I was able to function again. If I could manage to not project into the future, a future without one of my children, then perhaps I could make it day-by-day. As I was able to do this, life became a little easier.

As published in the Tigard Times on June 8, 1995

Graduation, A Reminder of Family's Loss

What should we do? We, the bereaved parents whose sons and daughters would have been graduating this school year. Do we go to the ceremony, where our hearts will be ripped out but also where we have invested years of our child's life? Do we listen to the remembrance and dedication of our child that many schools will have? Or do we stay home and hurt and wonder "Did they remember?"

This is such a personal and hard decision that changes from one moment to the next and will probably change again the day of the graduation ceremony. How will Alex's peers and their parents react to the sad faces of his two parents? Will they ignore our pain on this joyous day for their child or will they incorporate our pain into the day and wish him to be there with us all. I know he will be there, but not in the way we all wish.

Will we be greeted with open arms; kindness and understanding of our need for closure about his school life? Will they wish we had just stayed home? Would they realize that a person never knows when they might become us? I have certainly found out that there are no guarantees in life (as have the families of Oklahoma City.) Will we actually be able to go? I don't know.

When your child dies it is like you lose your place and society does not want to let you back in line. My constant dilemma at this point of fourteen months is can I face it...the 'it' being the judgment of society—or do I stay within my now insulated world, protected from hurt and people that truly don't understand the cruel pain of living in this world without my child.

In June many families in Portland, who I now know personally, will face this same dilemma. In Tigard, will the Huber's be able to go and see the culmination of what would have been Alex's school life at Tualatin High?

Whether we go or not, it will be a painful decision. We only have best wishes for all of Alex's classmates of many years (some all the way back to kindergarten) and hope they will understand the dilemma. We are truly thankful to the Class of '95 and all they have done for us. Alex will be with you. I hope we can be.

(This is also written in honor of Brad Sattler who would have graduated this year and his parents whose pain mirrors our own.)

10 A DRESSER FULL OF SOCKS

I recently had to face his books. This was almost the worst. Alex and I shared a love of reading and even a few books. He had become a somewhat sophisticated reader, but really preferred the world of fantasy. I didn't care for fantasy, but we both loved science fiction, particularly *Star Trek* books. I remember many a debate about Spock. Alex was in the middle of one of these books when he died. In fact, it had been his Christmas present to me and it was now his turn to read it. I never removed his bookmark and am so sad that he didn't get to finish the book.

Alex had been in a transition phase when he died. We had finished an addition to the house just ten days prior to his death. This was a large bonus room, bedroom, and bathroom. At eight hundred square feet, it was almost like an apartment. While we had both boys in mind, the larger intent was for Alex to live in it while attending junior college, then Morgan would have it after Alex moved on.

He had just started moving his things in when the accident happened and hadn't even hung his posters yet. The bathroom was finished on the day he died. He never saw it completed. This area didn't truly have the Alex feel to it yet, but his old room had been converted into a music area for the piano and stereo. Perhaps this kept me from enshrining his bedroom and things. Also, his friends wanted to touch his clothes, hats and bedding, which I imagine brought a connection. Morgan rushed in and shooed everyone out and boxed up all the smaller stuff. He was protecting his brother.

During the week after the funeral, my mother-in-law had stripped Alex's bed and done all the household laundry. She was trying to be helpful, but what she did was destroy any fragrance of Alex. I was desolate. Then I remembered his P.E. clothes. I called the principal of his school, at home, early in the morning on the first day of spring break. This was three days after the funeral. I woke him up, but I didn't care. "Larry, please don't let anyone wash Alex's P.E. clothes in an effort to be kind. I need them." He rushed to the school and brought Alex's P.E. locker contents directly to me. Inside was the smelliest and dirtiest shirt I had ever seen. Had he been alive, I would have yelled at him for not bringing this home to be washed. But he wasn't alive and it had the scent of his sweat and cologne. To a grieving mother, there is not a more beautiful fragrance. This is carefully wrapped in plastic to preserve his smell. Whenever I feel a desperate need to know that he had been real, I pull out this shirt and hold it to my face. I don't do this very often anymore, but I know it is there when I need it.

For over a year, I didn't really do anything about his room. Morgan had absconded with his shirts, of which, I snatched back a few special ones. I didn't know what to do with everything. The thought of boxing it all up and putting it in the attic was appalling to me. I felt like I was denying his existence.

Then one day I read an article in a Compassionate Friends newsletter. Another bereaved mom had felt the same and had found a solution in the form of a cedar chest kept in her room. This was really the answer for me. I immediately bought a chest, which had two connected hearts carved on the front. This sits at the foot of our bed to this day. Over the course of another year I filled it with his things. It was very exhausting to do this and deal with the memories at the same time and unlike other chores, I could only manage little bits at a time.

There are some things that aren't in there, partly because of space. His underwear and socks still sit in his dresser drawers. I can't throw them away. I can't give them away. They are very personal items and every single time I look at them, I am driven back with pain. My son's underclothing did haunt me. Now they don't so much because we have arrived at a mutual understanding. They won't haunt me if I don't haunt them. I believe that they will be with me for the rest of my life. That is fine with me. As I have let go of other people's expectations, it is becoming easier to know that I can keep them. They aren't hurting anything sitting there. I don't look at them often. For some reason, I need to know that they are safe, not garbage. Maybe this validates that he really was here. I'll never really understand my emotions around his underwear, but these feelings do exist and I had to find a way to come to terms with them.

Three years after Alex died, Morgan moved into the bedroom and little apartment area. We are using his old room as our guestroom and have Alex's bedroom furniture in it. However, we had never removed his books from the nightstand and headboard bookshelf. Recently, my nephew came to live with us and we had to address this.

I held his childhood collection of *Little House on the Prairie* books and they tore at my heart. They were in excellent condition and had been a favorite of his. I remember giving them to him for Christmas one year. I put them on my bookshelf and read the collection, as he had always wanted me to.

Tucked in his nightstand sat his *Archie* comics. These are displayed at the checkout stand of the grocery store and whenever he was with me he'd beg for a new one. "Please Mom, would you get it for me?" I could never say "No." We packed these in a small box and put them in the closet by the dresser with his socks.

His desk was moved into my home office during the first year. I have gone through it, but everything remains as he had it. On rare occasions when I open the middle drawer, his checkbook looks up at me. It hurts. I can't look at it.

In about a year, we will be moving from this house we will have lived in for nine years. I don't know if I will need to transfer his things along with us and keep them near, or if I will have reached a point where I can let go of his dresser with the socks and his desk with the checkbook of pain. I do know I will let myself feel what is right for me and act accordingly.

Four Years Ago, Today

I sit quietly in the sunshine; I can't feel it.
I can see the colors; but they are so dull.
There are sounds; very dim, far away.
No brightness or hue or din
can penetrate
this loneliness, since
you left my side.
Oh, sweet son of mine
I miss your smile.
Your light has gone out
and I wander in this haze
trying to find my way.
I know you radiate in heaven.
Could you not send a
ray of sunshine
for me?

Terri Huber · 3/18/98

11

YOU CHANGED MY LIFE TODAY

Almost immediately after Alex died I felt the need to speak my pain and anger. I wanted to talk to the teens of the world and make them listen. My first attempt to implement this was at my son's high school. I phoned the principal, who had been friends with Alex and had spoken at his funeral, and imparted to him this wonderful idea. I knew I could make these kids listen and was determined it would be at Tualatin High School.

He certainly didn't respond as I had hoped and was quick to dash the possibility. Looking back, I can only imagine the sound of hysteria and anger in my voice. Plus, I didn't take into account his own grief with Alex's death. Of course, at that time I didn't take into account anyone else's grief. I had a huge chip on my shoulder and felt as if there wasn't another soul in the world who understood my pain.

My next attempt to actually speak was by invitation at eight months. I spoke, along with two other members of Compassionate Friends, to a classroom of ninth grade students. At the time, I felt that it went rather well. Looking back at the video, though, I saw this woman radiating anger and having a threatening posture toward the kids. I have since learned that kids, particularly teens, do not respond to lecturing, especially with this anger bias. Somehow I needed to talk to them instead of at them, bypass their ears and go right to the heart. At that point I did not have a clue how to do this.

Over the next eighteen months I went into intensive therapy, which I speak about in detail in another section. I worked through the intense anger and the many issues that surrounded my grief. At this point I was able to think a little more clearly and did some brainstorming about how it would be feasible to get into the high schools to convince these kids that they were vulnerable. I contacted M.A.D.D., Mothers Against Drunk Driving who put on what is called "Sober-Grad Programs" in conjunction with the Oregon State Patrol. Even though Alex had not been drinking or on drugs, my research had shown that more teens die from dangerous driving. I approached them from the perspective of saving lives from all angles. They felt this to be realistic and invited me to speak at a local high school. This particular high school is in our community and many, many students knew Alex personally or of his death. He died about six blocks from Tigard High School.

This time I would be prepared. I asked for feedback from my therapy support group. These people were extremely honest and helped me arrive at a way to get past the ears to the heart. The students needed to feel my pain to connect with my words. All I really needed to do was tell my story.

It worked! So many of these young men and women came to me afterward, in tears, and told me how my story impacted them. One young lady said, "I never want my mother to go through what you have." Another said, "You changed my life today," and yet another, "I will always remember your son." The staff was also moved and told me so. Most surprising to me were the emotions of the police officers. Several of them had been at the scene of Alex's accident and were visibly touched by my part in this story.

I have since had the opportunity to speak at over twenty different high schools. While the story at the core remains the same, I have learned how to incorporate Alex's life and the true message of why I am there in a manner that appears most effective. The students pay close attention, never making a sound except for tears. They look closely at his picture as I tell them, "This could be you." "He was like you, living his life, loving pizza and pop; girls and cars and phones and friends. He did not plan to die that day." "Do not make your family and friends come to your funeral." I feel as if for that moment they really get it. I hope so.

I always leave these schools with a sense of accomplishment. This, for me, comes from having remembered my son in a public manner, sharing his personality, life, and death. Although extremely fatigued, I usually complete these sessions with the hope that maybe in this group of kids no one will die from dangerous behavior, either behind the wheel or otherwise.

I have not regretted my decision to reach out in this manner. I am grateful for this opportunity and feel that it has helped me move forward in assimilating my grief in a manner that I can learn to live with. Speaking to these young people allows me to verbalize my own pain and perhaps spare another family the agony of this type of loss. However, every year I evaluate my situation and reconsider whether to continue. While I have spoken about all the good from it, there is a downside.

I have to revisit the car crash in mind and heart every time I speak. The students need to hear about it to connect with the reality of the situation. But it never gets easy to talk about and is always an emotional experience. The kids have all witnessed my tears. These lectures have caused me sleepless nights with reawakened waves of grief, large waves. For now, the positive outweighs the negative and I will continue until I feel that the negative consequences, for me, have become too heavy to carry.

12 MY FAITH IN GOD

Not for a single instance did my faith in a loving God waiver. I did find it to be sometimes interesting, other times irritating, and yet oftentimes touching that so many of my friends and acquaintances did not seem to think this was good enough.

Almost from the day Alex died people were offering their interpretations of why this would happen in God's world. They did it in a variety of ways: "God only takes the best"; "God saved him from pain in the future"; "It was meant to be." Most of this sort of thing was very hurtful and did not make sense to me. I would just nod my head and go about the business of surviving.

Others were more persistent. One casual acquaintance hounded me to give her time to share her philosophy that I should not mourn because I would again see Alex in Heaven. This was definitely a person who had her own agenda. She was so uncomfortable with my grief, that she wanted it to be over—six whole weeks after we buried Alex. After this conversation I never heard from her again.

Another casual acquaintance offered to take me to her church. This offer was made with such love and such an attempt to understand my pain that I found it the most touching and the most difficult to ignore.

After three attempts on her part, she said to me, "How about I let you come to me if you would like to attend my church." This was very helpful and took the burden of trying to turn her down in a positive way off my shoulders. We have become close friends and have learned to respect each other's personal relationship with God. She does not know the pain of losing a child to death and does not attempt to explain it, trivialize it, or take the grief away. Her offer had been made from the heart in an effort to help soothe my heart, and I will always appreciate the intent.

My faith has become even deeper than before. I believe my son to be with God in a place that I cannot even conceive of. This, however, does not take away my grief. Grief is about Alex not being here, about missing him and wanting to hold him in my arms, about talking with him, about all the things parents do every day and are now denied me.

Alex, he is just fine in heaven. I'm the one that is not fine. Now it takes all I have in me to try to survive here on this earth. I pray for strength and I talk to my son constantly. I believe that he is watching over his family and friends and sends love and strength. Many people have organized prayer groups for our family and I believe this has also helped. After all, I am still in the land of the living and I didn't think that I would be. Something has helped me and I choose to believe that it is God, love from others, and my precious Alex.

Tears Fall

The tears fall
silently
down my face.
Have they stopped
even for an
instant?
I mourn & cry
and it seems
unending,
but...
how can it end?
For
I will always
cry about
my
Alex
and I will
always miss him.

Terri Huber · 12/7/95

13 *Premonitions and Signs*

I had never been a person to believe in premonitions or signs from above and assorted other paranormal things. I didn't realize until the death of Alex what I had been experiencing was just that.

A year before Alex died my dear friend's daughter died in a vehicle accident much the same as Alex's would be. I hurt so badly for her. Laurie and I had been friends over twenty-five years, since I was about fifteen years old and she was fourteen. I'll never forget the morning she called and told me that Elizabeth was dead. I was putting on mascara, such a normal activity. I couldn't begin to imagine her pain; little did I know.

For the next several months I was in a deep depression and attributed this to the death of this beautiful child. Laurie and her family lived in a different state, so I didn't know her children well and my family was a bit alarmed at my state of mind. I knew my friend well, though, and I hurt as I witnessed her pain.

I started having dreams that one of my boys would die. I walked around with this feeling that something was going to happen. When my father died of terminal cancer in July of that year, I thought maybe this was my dread, but it didn't lift. In September I was sure I was going to die and wrote letters to the boys, just in case. Also in September a local boy, Brad, died in an auto accident right by our home. He was a classmate of Alex's and they had known each other. His father was Morgan's teacher.

I couldn't get these people off my mind. I would ask the teachers I knew about Leo, Brad's father, and how he was doing. Right before Thanksgiving I felt compelled to write to this man and tell him that Alex had known and liked Brad, and how very sorry I was about his death. The gesture was out of character for me. I didn't know this man his wife. I felt this compulsion, despite this. Both Leo and Barb came to Alex's funeral, four months later, and went on to become our close friends. Leo died in a motorcycle accident 2½ years after his son died.

Oddly enough, after I got through the first few of weeks following Alex's death, I knew his loss to be what was causing the dread, because it had lifted. I was able to tell the difference between the horrible grief and that feeling that something was about to happen. I was also grateful for all those feelings before, because they made me realize that if there were nothing more in life than just our bodies, I wouldn't have had these feelings. These mini-premonitions I know to have been God's way of preparing me for what was to come, yet to also let me know He would be by my side throughout. I thought, "Okay, if I knew in advance then there has to be a God and that means Alex is with him. I will see him again." It was a comfort knowing that somewhere in me I had this knowledge.

I then deduced that if I knew in advance of his impending death then maybe some sign would come my way showing that he is around. I'd notice his name everywhere. At the time, Alexander was not a common name, but I saw it constantly. Not much evidence for someone else, but it sure helped me at the time.

On May 15, 1994 (exactly two months after he died) I had my first dream about Alex. This dream and the subsequent ones all had a different feel and texture than normal dreams. They made sense, were in color and I could feel and smell things. I was sure that I was with my boy and that he was letting me know that he was all right. Didn't matter a lot to me that other people might have a different interpretation. I was there and knew the intensity of these visits.

Four months after Alex died the most preeminent sign happened for me. I was in a particularly bad emotional condition that day. I wanted to protect John from this rawness, so I went into our bedroom walk-in closet. There was a shirt of Alex's hanging in there; I grabbed it and hung on for dear life. I was doubled over in pain and sobbing when all of a sudden I heard a couple of musical notes. Surprisingly, I wasn't shocked. In fact, I remember saying, "All right Alex, I hear you."

The music had come from a thirty-year-old jewelry box that had been broken for years. I reached up high to a back corner of the closet, took it down, and tried to make it play again and could not. The knob on the back was loose and just spun in circles. My son had made music from a broken music box to let me know he was near. This has been the biggest comfort I have had since he died, bar none.

Can I prove to others that all of this is true and do I need to? No. I believe my son to be near, and with the grace of God, watching over all who love him.

14 *PSYCHICS*

Alex had only been dead a week when another bereaved parent gave me a book about a psychic medium, George Anderson. I let it lay around for about three weeks and then in a moment of abject despair, I picked it up and read it. It changed my grieving life.

I had always, sort of, believed in psychic phenomenon, but hadn't any real interest in pursuing it. I hadn't had anyone die, in my life, where I had trouble coming to grips with the grief. My father had died nine months prior and I did love him, but the difference between my grief for him and grief for my son is voluminous. My dad had lived sixty-seven years and Alex only had seventeen years. Besides, losing a child is out of order. While I would never discount the grief of another over anyone they have lost—I had to learn this—for me the death of my son was my worst loss.

When I read this book about George, for the first time, I felt hope. I did some research, read other books about him and then decided that not only was he legitimate, but I was going to see him. That he had a several-year waiting list meant absolutely nothing to me. Nor did the fact that many important people in my life objected for either religious reasons or fear that he was a charlatan. I knew I would see him and my pursuit began. My reason to live had presented itself.

For a period of six months I pursued every avenue for ways to contact him for an appointment. I truly believe that I was guided in my efforts—by Alex—because of how it simply fell into my lap. Within eight months of Alex's death, I was sitting in a room with George in Alabama and having a conversation with my son.

Not a shred of doubt in my mind or heart exists that I was in contact with Alex. Although I cried through the entire hour-long visit, I was absolutely elated. Alex's personality came shining through along with facts that only he could know. I also found George to be spiritual and non-threatening; gentle and kind; a wonderful conduit through whom God worked to bring my son to me. I believe with every fiber of my being that God granted me this gift, to help me through my grief. A few naysayers even reconsidered after hearing the tape of my session

There is a downside, however. I had said and had expected that when I reached Alex, my grief would disappear, evaporate. If I knew he was okay then I wouldn't be so sad and suicidal anymore. I was wrong! My grief abated for about two weeks and then I went into a major depressive crash. What I came away with, I had already known. Alex really is fine. Despite my belief in the hereafter and his continued life, I still missed him and wanted him here.

I do not regret my venture to see George. I later went to see James Van Praague, who is here on the West Coast. To me both appear to be decent men with a wonderful mission. I know seeing them was merely a piece of the path toward where I now am, though I had considered it to be the whole path. I am grateful and hold them close in my prayers, particularly George.

My quest to see him gave me a mission in life, which kept me on this earth for that time. I did not care what anyone else thought because I knew what I needed to do to save my sanity. I am not ashamed or embarrassed, and while not every bereaved parent seeks out this sort of comfort, many do.

No one can know the despair of losing a child to death, unless they have had the misfortune to experience it. I ask those non-bereaved parents who are critical to hold their opinions. Unless your child has died, you don't know for sure what you would do. I have stood next to evangelical Christians, Catholics, Mormons, and Jews, all of who were seeking George or another like him. I am not encouraging any one to do this, though. It was a personal choice for me and I was grateful for the opportunity. George was clear that my visit could help a little, but it would not take away my grief. I didn't believe him. I now do.

George Anderson Web Page—www.georgeanderson.com

James Van Praague Web Page—www.vanpraagh.com

15 MY SMALL GROUP

It's funny how some of the most significant things in life happen without planning of any kind. Some of my greatest learning experiences have come about like this.

I returned from Alabama in November 1994, after seeing George Anderson, and felt very light and happy. I told everyone I could think of and invited them to listen to the tape of the session. The word started to get out around The Compassionate Friends and the interest in hearing the tape was high. Two of us bereaved moms had gone together and we each had a tape of our own session. Many bereaved parents will look for comfort in many ways. Obviously, the people interested had no inhibitions about psychic contact.

An evening was arranged for grieving parents to come to my house and listen to the tapes. This was neither sponsored by, nor part of The Compassionate Friends organization. Five grieving women came to hear. At the time, I think the longest bereaved was about two and one-half years, so we were still very fresh in our grief.

This time was representative of tentative friendships and hope. These women had friends who were interested, too, so we arranged to meet again in about a month and that time there were eight of us. After listening to our tapes we discussed how to get everyone to George Anderson. During this same meeting the name of James Van Praague was introduced to us and we listened to a tape of a sitting with him. We were extremely impressed.

We thought it might be helpful to get together again and talk about our kids and keep apprised of new information about George and James. Originally, we would just meet at my house, but after the first six months we expanded to other homes. Over potluck meals we grew to know each other and develop a bond of affection and trust. We were on a mission for everyone to have the opportunity to see George.

Our group would spend time together during the holiday season, which was almost unbearable. Two of the women lost their children at Christmastime, rendering the holiday their own particular hell. The rest of us also had to face Christmas without our child and together we forged through this and relied on each other. When my family went away for Christmas, I would look at a group photo of these moms and it would provide strength, especially through that second Christmas.

While it had never been so planned, we ended up staying with the original group of eight women. We never did find a name for our group, so it remained the "Small Group." By the time others were interested in becoming a part of it we had forged some tight bonds and felt newcomers would feel left out. Fortunately, many of them went on to form their own small groups.

Our group stayed together for about two years. We had accomplished our mission for everyone interested to see George and then later, James. We had helped each other along in this pursuit and in times of need

I am not exactly sure why we slowly drifted apart. Perhaps it was that our interests had been primarily in this psychic pursuit and our only other common ground was the death of our children. As we started to move forward in life, our personalities started to reassert and mixed feelings arose in me. I felt some hurt and found myself staying away. Already filled with so much hurt I couldn't face anymore.

My involvement with them facilitated some huge growth experiences and gave me a safe place to grieve. I am very grateful to have known these women and to have been part of their lives, even for awhile. I remain close to two of them. Susan and I have a love of reading and share a common view of the world. Barbara (BJ) is Brad's mom and our friendship started before the group formed and continued after it dissolved.

My time with all of them was special and helped me along on my path. I am learning that everything is just for a time, though, and this is yet another reason for me to stay in the moment.

My Small Group—Thank you to Barbara, Susan, Carol, Annette, Renee, Dodie and Patricia (now deceased). You will always be in my heart.

A Door Was Opened

I stand on the edge of eternity's doorstep,
Across the threshold the precipice beckons
But the correct path is not marked!

Yet, you crossed eternity's threshold,
A door quickly opened and you were on your way.
Where was your path that leads to the light?
Why can't you show me the way?

Now, days are much too long,
And my nights grow shorter,
Reality fades,
Then blossoms in earnest.
We search, and we struggle
For the meaning of normal.

Empty feelings,
Does the heart still beat?
Weave and wander,
What path my feet?

Blind to the path,
I see not light
Must I stay and live earth's plight?
When will this testing be complete?

J. P. Huber · 3/94

16 *FORGIVENESS*

I don't believe I have totally forgiven Alex. This is such a difficult thing to know, much less admit to anyone else. I try, I really do. Some days when I think about the accident I tell myself, "He was just being a teenager and doing what so many do. Other days it's "How could he do this to us—he knew better." Then I go into feelings of anger and what might have been.

I'm not as rough on myself anymore about this because I have come to realize that forgiveness is a process, not an absolute. A person can forgive deep in her heart, one day, and the next something will trigger a feeling and the anger and despair reasserts.

Certainly, my feelings of being unable to forgive Alex are not nearly as intense as they were in the beginning. I know in my heart that he wants me to forgive him, without reservation. I also absolutely believe that it was his time to go but can't transcend feeling betrayed by his behavior and I do not know that this will ever totally resolve itself. I pray for help; I yell at him in my journals; I try to let go. I think this all helps a little and maybe one day I will have arrived at that place of total forgiveness. I hope so because it feels like the right thing for me.

The other person I need to forgive is myself. There is a part of me that still feels responsible for his death. I should have gone to the school when the urge struck that day; I should have known; I should have talked more, and on and on. The should-haves haunted me for the longest time. I thought a good mother does not let her child die or if she does, she should die too. I have worked through the biggest portion of this guilt, but I can't dwell on it, ever, or all the should-haves rear up, which can take me back to the edge of despair.

I don't look back to that time very much anymore. After four and a half years I do have some control about where my thoughts go. Even when I am experiencing a grief attack, I no longer go there in my head. I still grieve and miss Alex, and it would be easy to do, but I don't see a future for myself if I dwell in the land of what-if and despair. I try to think of who he was and how he lived as opposed to his death. I am successful a good portion of the time.

I am in my future and it will be what I make it, through my memories, my love of family and friends, my hope of seeing Alex again, and staying in the moment; be what it may.

Life and Death

Never to be the same,
Events, labeled, have no meaning,
Pale, in dawn's cruel light.

Eagles soar
Lions roars,
Hearts torn in pain.

As rain beats down,
Soaks the ground,
No footsteps will disturb.

Life's river flows,
But I hesitate,
Caught in quiet eddies.

To reflect on love,
I dream and pause,
Time, ease the pain?

The river tugs
Can I be strong?
Yet, I am to wonder

Oh, memories,
Fond memories,
Leave me strength?

Quiet echoes,
Love remembered
Sail on to your new purpose!

J. P. Huber · 3/19/94

17
MORGAN, MY SON

I can't even begin to imagine what it must be like for Morgan. One minute he is thirteen years old and has a happy and normal family life, which included a mom, dad and an older brother. The next moment he is thrust into a world of despair, anger, and disbelief. Granted we were all in that same place, but we weren't thirteen years old, a mere baby.

Morgan may, in some ways, have lost more than anybody. His brother died and he lost the parents he knew; we became shells of the people we had been, shells that cried all the time. Over the course of the next six months both his grandmothers walked away and at four years we have never heard from them again. His aunts, my sisters, also walked away and took with them his cousins who would have been a lifeline. Morgan ended up without any family, trying to cope with parents who had become overprotective and barely recognizable. My poor son, I am so sorry.

We are very proud of who he has become despite such terrible trauma. Many kids that are thrust into traumatic situations turn to drugs, alcohol, violence, or suicide. Morgan turned to his music. He had always been a singer and we realized his talent when he was as young as two years old. Throughout elementary school he stood out as a soloist and yet this never went to his head. As with his brother, he is kind and generous and gentle. He does not see music as a way to compete or try to be better than the next person, but as a way to express himself, and during this time, to express his grief. Morgan recorded the song *Somewhere Out There*, the night before Alex's funeral and it was the music we used. The words were perfect and when he sang, "And even though I know how very far apart we are, it helps to think we might be wish-in' on the same bright star," it felt as if this song had been written for this moment.

One year after Alex's death, Morgan was in eighth grade and had the opportunity to choose his own solo to perform in the school concert. He chose *Tears in Heaven* by Eric Clapton, who had written this to honor his young son who died from a fall. We know Morgan partially chose this for his dad and I, but I also think he did it for himself as another way to express grief and mourning and missing of his elder brother.

The school had been concerned that this song might not be appropriate, but eventually came to the conclusion that it would facilitate Morgan's own healing. In the wake of the Oklahoma bombing and several teachers who were bereaved parents, this song brought about a bonding of hearts. Morgan was asked to reprise it at the end of the year assembly in front of the student body of eight hundred peers. He helped create a very special moment, which also helped his own grief.

Morgan has continued on with his music through high school and is a stand out performer. He has had many solos, but I have to admit that his first solo of *Moon River* in ninth grade is my favorite memory. I watched him and thought "One of my dreams has come true. My son is on that high school stage." Alex had been the actor and Morgan the singer and my wish was that one day they would be on the this school stage. Morgan was there and watching him made me feel some hope for my own future. I felt the quickening of joy for the first time since my precious Alex had died.

Morgan recently said that the drawback of being a competent singer is that people only liked him for his voice. That is not true. People respect Morgan profoundly for his gift and the joy it brings, but love him for who his is, a funny, gentle, kind, and compassionate young man.

Morgan is now eighteen-years-old, older than his older brother ever became. Another cross to bear and challenge to meet, but he is doing it, with all the grace possible for one so young. His aunts, uncles, and cousins have come back into his life and ours. New relationships are being built. Particularly good to watch are the bonds being forged between his cousin, Bill, Alex's peer, and Morgan. So healing for both of them. Another joy for me to witness as I collect all these little joys and try to soothe my own shattered heart.

TIME

You see it as trees,
you see it as animals
you see it as the sea
you see it overhead.

You see it as a rock,
you can touch it.
But its something that
will never come again.
It passes by like the
waves of the ocean
and disappears; but
you remember it.

You see it all around
you think it's there forever,
but disappears
as do voices
in the wind.

It's there always.
You can't run from it,
you can't hide from it,
it's there,
forever and always,
it's there.

Morgan Huber
10/96

18
TOGETHER IN GRIEF

"I would trade anyone's life to have Alex back." How could he ever forgive me for those words? Yet he did. My husband of twenty-seven years (as I write this) has suffered, grieved, and supported me, with the knowledge that I would rather anyone had died but one of our sons. I never specifically said that I wished he had died, but in my grief, I continued to say, "Anybody, anybody but Alex." As horrid as that sounds, he also knew that I wanted to be at the top that list. Anyone except Morgan.

These were the types of wild thoughts and words that came out of my mouth during the first few months after Alex died. Even then, I knew it didn't make sense, because there was no such thing as a trade, but it didn't matter. John stood by me and understood the depth of my despair. He would say "It was harder for you, the mom." I don't believe this to be true because I witnessed his suffering, but mine sure manifested differently than his. He never appeared to carry the anger that I did, which made his grieving process not quite so explosive.

My dear husband lived with the thought, everyday, that he could come home to a dead wife. He never doubted how much I wanted to go or how hard I was fighting to stay. I know that he knew I loved him and

Morgan but that I was desperate to see Alex and to not feel this excruciating pain any longer.

John did things for me that were somewhat out of character for him. He attended group meetings of Compassionate Friends and even endured group hugs, which I continue to tease him about; took classes about women in grief; read all the books I presented to him. Still loved me when I couldn't bear to be touched or consoled, my skin hurt all the time. I became hypersensitive to anyone's touch. He stood by me as I traveled around the country looking for answers. He has watched me flounder in despair and rage at the injustice of it all and accepted me as I went through change. He has cooked meal after meal for several years after working hard all day. He would find me crying in the middle of the kitchen because I couldn't decide what to cook or how to begin, so he just did it himself, for his family. He would call me a couple of times a day from work, just to see how I was doing. He would not get angry with me for not moving all day. Some days all I could do was stare at a wall or silent television. He worried, but he understood. Many times we would both watch cooking shows without any sound.

While John supported me in all the ways I tried to cope, he managed his own grief by writing poetry about our boy. His is a quieter grief. He is a calm and gentle man and Alex was turning out much like him. He is and was devastated but was able to find a perspective sooner than I. He could not fix my grief; he could not bring Alex back; he was helpless except where Morgan was concerned. He focused his love and attention where it was needed, in the here and now. While he certainly had times of intense pain, and still does, he could see a future before I could.

We had both just existed, he in his way and me in mine. Without question I think he gave more to me and all I could do was hold him in his tears and grief and never ask him to be strong for me, although he tried. I never lost sight of the fact that John, too, was robbed of his son. We grieved together but in different ways. For John, I stayed.

I am so grateful that he was and is my husband and together we bore this child. Together we mourn him. We are finding a new rhythm to our lives and while I will not minimize the hard work I have done, I know that much of it would not have been possible without him by my side. His continued love, support, and acceptance made all the difference for me.

19 SOMEDAY, THEY SAY

•It will not hurt anymore.

•You will see him again.

•Thanksgiving and Christmas will be joyful.

•You will have grandchildren.

•You will feel joy.

•You will smile instead of hurt, at the memories.

•You will be able to let go of those socks.

•You won't even remember the date of his death.

All these things may be true, but:

I may have grandchildren, whom I will love, but they will not replace Alex.

I feel joy many times now, but it is laid upon sadness.

The holidays will come and the holidays will go, joyful or not.

I smile at the memories even while I hurt.

I'm keeping the damn socks.

Forget the date of his death? Unlikely!

I will see him again, but that seems forever from now.

I may not be the raw wound I was at first, but I will always mind and I will always hurt when I think of my Alex not being here.

20 TIME TO MOVE ON

Alex was gone only six weeks and it started. "Time to move on. Mustn't wallow in sadness because Alex wouldn't want it." They said it—oh so many them. I couldn't even breathe and was still in the midst of panic attacks. *Not grieve; move on; what does that mean? I'm actually getting out of bed. Isn't that good enough for now? My son is dead and I feel as if I died, also. Leave me alone.*

I don't remember months two, three, four and five, but I remember six. The effects of all the well-meaning and hurtful comments rose up in me, and I exploded in the form of an article. I lashed out at the do-gooders who wanted to fix me. They hadn't lost a child, but they sure had the answers for me. "He's with God and that should be good enough for you."

I was enraged, but as always, I swallowed it until nothing more would go down. Six months, he was still gone, and it hurt, maybe even more than before. How could people be so cruel? If they thought it was so glorious that Alex was in heaven, perhaps they would like to offer up their child. Of course, this statement didn't go over very well, but it was made during my very angry period. The article was published and I was left alone for awhile.

By ten months I increasingly heard; "Terri it is time to move on." *What does that mean? I am moving on, but are they saying that they want me to forget and not mourn? How could I do that? How could any parent? I am creating a new me, but it takes time.* I wrote another article about moving on.

I'm doing it world, but give me a break. My son is dead, not away at college. It takes time to adjust to never seeing him again. (I know I will see him when I die but that is not the same as the here and now.) Understand, please, that we, the bereaved parents of the world, have had our hearts torn from our bodies and the pain is intolerable. We must re-grow a new one and it will still be missing a part.

Two years, three years, four years. "What? Your son died. How awful! Did it happen recently?" they would ask.

"No. I know it sounds like a long time," I would once again answer, "but it still feels like yesterday and at the same time seems like forever since I held him."

"Shouldn't you get help? You must be neglecting your other son," they would accuse, using that tone which indicated how much better they would do if they were me. "After all, it has been a long time and it is not good to be so absorbed in a dead person. You should move on."

"I do not neglect Morgan. I am moving on, but I mourn. I will live, but I mourn. I will love, but I mourn. I will laugh, and I will still mourn. I will also cry and cry very probably, until the day I die, but I will have had a life."

Many people appear to think that moving on means never saying his name again, or crying over the pain of his absense. They want to be comfortable in my presense and for many the vocalization of my loss definitely excludes this. I believe moving on means learning to actually live a full life while having this pain in it. I am doing it but on my own time line, not in the period they have allotted.

It is a good life that has a wonderful husband and son in it. We had the joy of Alex in our lives. I am blessed with true and devoted friends. With all of this, I will still mourn, but is that not part of it? I love you, Alex.

21 HOW COULD YOU?

"How could you have contemplated suicide? What a horrid and cruel thing to do to your family."

I've had these words spoken to me as I struggled through severe, debilitating grief and depression. I don't recall ever contemplating suicide. I didn't sit with my chin resting in my hand logically thinking through the pros and cons.

"You must have lost your faith in God to ever consider this option."

No, I never lost my faith. In fact, it was probably just that which stopped me in the end. I don't know. What I do know is that I wasn't thinking about faith or even being with Alex.

At the time of this intense agony of my soul, I did not think of my family or the pain for them. I did not think of my friends. I did not think. I doubled over in agony and wanted it all to end. I did not feel capable of continuing on. I existed in a black hole of agonizing pain and I could not see that it would stop. I was like an animal screaming in agony. Had I been a horse, I would have been euthanized, but as a human being I had to feel it, deal with it, endure it, and finally come through it. I know that God understood. What a shame that so many people didn't even try.

Eighteen months after the accident was the last time I allowed myself to sink to this level of despair. I was actually on my way to get the sleeping pills that had been prescribed early on in my bereavement and were never taken, when suddenly, a life-size portrait of Morgan's face appeared in my mind. This was very unusual for me, as I had never before seen pictures in my head. Wherever this came from, be it from God, from Alex, or simply from my inner resources, it stopped me cold in my tracks. I knew that Morgan could not come home and find the body of his mother. I went to the phone and started dialing friends for help. I started at the top of my emergency list and followed it down until someone answered. My friend probably saved my life that day through her understanding and compassion.

Since then, I never allowed myself to go into that black hole again. I think about how I can live each day and will not add more pain to my family's life. I started to use the tool that has since become a fundamental part of my life; *stay in the moment.*

When I grieve, I stay in that moment and never again project that the continuation of my my pain and despair will last at this level, into forever. I must only get through five minutes at a time. Using this method does ease me through that dangerous time and I am able to once again breathe. I have never again contemplated suicide, but I am vigilant to not let myself go that low. The attitude and the words stay *in the moment* kept me going from then on.

One outside influence that also helped was the addition of anti-depressents in my life. I had been one of the many that thought these drugs were not for me and they would disconnect me from the grief over my son. I had tried them early on in my despair and anxiety and had a serious depressive reaction. Due to this I did not try another type for four years, at which time I went to a psychiatrist and experimented in a much better dosage controlled situation. While I had resolved the suicide feelings by that time, I was still very depressed and not able to function. These anti-depressents got me out of my chair and enabled me to go about the business of everyday matters. They did not relieve my mourning of Alex or make me feel drugged. I am on this medication still and grateful for the assistance in managing my life.

That I have resolved this suicide issue in my heart and mind does not mean I have total resolution to Alex's premature death. Part of me believes in the spiritual implication of "It was his time." Another part of me, the mother part, still wails at the injustice and wants an answer. I am still searching for that answer and for peace of spirit.

22 *IF THIS WERE A FAIRY TALE*

If this were a fairy tale I could, possibly, live happily ever after, even without Alex. That is not how it works, though. I have dealt with the debilitating parts of grief, but I will always mourn the death of my firstborn. John will always mourn the death of his firstborn. Morgan will always mourn the death of his brother and only sibling, whom he knew for a short thirteen years.

If this were any other kind of story, this story of my path of grief, I could be so grateful for what I do have that I would not mourn what I have lost. I am grateful for my husband, my son, my sisters, and my friends and for the privilege of having had Alex in my life for even a few short years. We are financially stable so I was able to quit work and find a way to survive the premature death of my son. I am grateful, but I hurt anyway. I thank God, but I mourn. I love all of these people, but they do not take Alex's place in my life. He was unique, as is each of us.

Despite finding a certain degree of happiness, moments of joy, and contentment in the moment, the feeling that all is right in my world is no longer possible. This world can never be right, for me, without my eldest son. But I am still here. I am still a mother to Alex and Morgan. I am still a wife. I am creating a new life, and in so doing try to live it in a way that will honor my son. I am trying to be a better person, so that he will be proud of me for carrying forward. I will one day see him again and I hope he can say, "You did good, Ma."

23 OCEAN OF FOREVER

Mesmerized and staring at the great waves that roll in, I can't look away. These breakers slap the sand in fury and then lay down as gentle as kittens to go back home to the sea.

This great Pacific Ocean seems to have been here forever in its vastness. Its colors change as if it, too, is a rainbow of another kind. When the sun is bright, the ocean sparkles in different shades of blue and green; and when the clouds roll in, it takes on the somberness of gray. Perhaps it needs days of sadness and days of cheer, also. When a storm is brewing, the waves are large and angry, whipping and rolling, trying to go somewhere and not as interested in going home. I can relate. I bring my woes to you, mighty sea, knowing you cannot take them away, but you can help me witness forever.

You were here when I was not. You have seen life and death. If you could think, what would your thoughts be of mankind? Through your whimsy and your fury are you showing me that life goes on, no matter what? I think I knew that, but I needed you to show me.

I have come to you in joy and flitted and played with you and others in the fullness of the sunny day. I relish those times and can remember them vividly. I have come to you in despair and tried to remember a reason for living. I watched your waves and knew that no matter what, they would be here and remain as testament to the world.

I have come to you in sadness and written a story in your sand. I thought that when you came into shore and washed my story away, it would make me even sadder, but the opposite happened. As you took it out to the vastness of forever, I knew it would still exist, just in another form. Such surprising comfort this gave me, symbolizing Alex's path from one type of life into another.

Oh, mighty sea of life, you will be here when I am gone, and one day it will no longer matter that my son left this world prematurely, because I will be with him.

JOURNALS

March 26, 1994
Dear Alex,

It has been 11 days since you left us, and I still don't believe it. I want to turn back the clock and make this okay. Stop the accident. How could you speed, son? I want to be mad at you, but I know that you felt in total control and, as Aunt Cindy has said many times, you did not plan to die.

I keep seeing this accident and seeing your beautiful self and I want to go with you, or better yet, instead of you. But we have to be here for little brother. Thank goodness you hugged and harrassed him good-bye—remember I tried to stop you, but you were so funny. Of course, he was a growly bear, but you told him he was cute and you left happy.

If I was mad at you it was for deliberately putting two kids in the car and deliberately leaving school, when we had discussed this. I know you were a good kid and that boys do things like this, but you got caught. I always told you that you would get caught. But not like this. I hope you are with Elizabeth. And my grandma died on Monday—maybe she is with you.

You wouldn't have believed the service. Over 500 people were there. You have so many friends. Did you know how many? I know how nice you were, but obviously you were even nicer and kinder to other people than we realized.

I miss you so much, honey. Dad and I cry and hurt for you. For me I want to hold you and pat your hair, feel you sides. Dad feels guilty. He thinks we could have talked harder and made you listen. But you and I both know how stubborn you are. I know you get that from me. Invincible. Unafraid. It can't happen to you. I am so sorry we couldn't make you realize the danger. I'm so sorry. I love you, I love you, I love you. We miss you. Help Brother. He's trying to be strong. He sang to you at the service. You would have been nuts to hear *Somewhere Out There* again, but this time you would have liked it.

Your school and friends are doing so many nice things for us, and you:
1995 Alex Huber Scholarship Fund
A large donation from Mentor Graphics to The Feingold Association
An empty chair in your honor at graduation ceremonies
A plaque in the track field, surrounded by inscribed bricks
The first track meet of each year is the Alex J. Huber track meet
Your locker will be memorialized with your things inside, including your last Star Trek book and sealed with a clear plexi-glass door.

The poems written for you will be silk-screened and sold with the proceeds going to the your scholarship fund.

You and we are so loved. I, for one, have by far underestimated people. We won't do that anymore.

March 27, 1994
Dear Alex,

I just watched a Rabbi Kushner talk on TV about why bad things happen to good people. It is hard to process. I don't know what or how to think. He seems to be a nice man who has had tragedy. Can you help me? I need so badly to feel your presence. I think it could give me a peace that would forever help. Try, honey.

Last evening I really fell apart again. It felt just like someone had told me that this had just happened all over again. Can we survive without you? Do we want to? No—Do we have too? Yes. The feeling I had was panic. I couldn't imagine never holding you again and was looking for you. How could this have happened? It is not possible that you are no longer with us. I have always believed that all things happen for a reason. But I think this time it will be impossible to find, and even if I do it won't matter.

Your friend, Glen, phoned last night and we spoke for some time. He calls you perfect. You and I both know that is not true, but I think you were his idea of a perfect friend. You were always there and you didn't smoke or drink or do drugs. You are so admired for this. I miss you so much.

I love you.

April 13, 1994

I just got back from the cemetery and it is so hard to see you there, to know that I could dig and find your body. I want to hold you so badly. I am considering so many things, like the medium George Anderson. I need to talk to you and have you answer. I do feel like you sang to me on Monday night while I was sleeping and I want to be thankful for even that, but I need more. Is there any way for me to find peace? I've always been such a take-charge and take-care-of-business sort of person, and I feel helpless and hopeless right now. How do I get through this?

My counselor, Susan, wants to put me on anti-depressants, but I am not sure. What do I do? Feeling like this all the time hurts so bad, but I'm afraid I'll move away from you emotionally if I take them. This grief seems to continue to tie me to you. Alex, please help me. You are such a wise young man and have always been there for everyone. Can you not find a way to be there for me, too. Please.

I love you.

April 16, 1994
Dear Alex,

I feel like I am going crazy. I am so overwhelmed with the need to see you that I feel like I will blow up. Sometimes I do OK because I know you are safe and warm and know I love you, but today it doesn't help. Where do I put this need? Little Brother can only take so much and I don't know what to do. People offer to help, but no one can help, not really. Living the rest of my life like this seems impossible. Please help me, Son.

May 2, 1994
Dear Alex,

Monday's are always hard for some reason. I feel on the edge of panic again tonight. Just as I was starting to panic a friend phoned. I was able to be somewhat calm for that conversation, but now I feel quivery and headachy. Oh, my Alex, why can't I reach you? Your dad says he thinks you came to him when he was under anesthesia during surgery, and now he feels a little lighter. Did you, my boy? Are you not able to reach me? I can see you trying. Please keep trying.

May 15, 1994
Dear Alex,

Today is two whole months since you were killed. Unbelievable. I didn't expect to be alive on this day. How is it possible that life has continued on without you here? I thought that I saw you last night in my dreams. You just looked at me, for a long time. I feel that you need to tell me something or perhaps my wish to communicate to you is so strong that I am imposing this need on you, and it is not true. I know my need to talk to you is overwhelming, and I am on a search to find you. I need to hold you in my dreams and feel your presence again. Oh, Alex I miss you.

What do I miss? The "Hi, Ma"! The teasing and loping for food in the kitchen, the constant use of your phone, the comments to Little Bro, the love for your cat, Millie and especially the ruffled hair (of mine) every time you walked by. There are so many small things. I want to stroke your hair and smell your scent and feel your hands on my shoulders. See your mess in the bathroom. How can I not see you again in this lifetime? I need to so badly and I can't. I cannot even begin to believe that I am not hysterical right this minute. We are all so lonely without you.

Please come to all of us in our dreams. I don't think you get tired over there and we need you so badly now. You can rest later, and we will let you move on when some healing is done. I love you my long, lean, and lanky #1 son (in birth order-not my heart). But you will always be in my heart. You are with me every minute.

May 28, 1994

I don't know how to describe how I feel today. It has been 10 weeks and 4 days since you left us for the other side. I can't believe it has been so long since I have hugged you and yelled at you for dinner or heard your voice. I will probably watch a tape of you soon. I need to hear your voice.

I ordered a special lattice arrangement of irises and baby white carnations for your grave. Your headstone came in last week. It is so hard to look at because you look so alive and vital and beautiful. It does give me comfort to know that people will see a person and not just an anonymous name. Many years from now people will see your face. But I can't think of many years from now because just today is very difficult. I still go see you about every day. Yesterday I put a glass blue bird on your stone. It is a gift from me, just because. For some reason, that bird symbolizes something about you, so it belongs to you.

I so wish I could end it all. The only reason I am staying around is Morgan and Dad, and I really believe I would have to witness their suffering if I chose to kill myself. It would be another kind of hell. I can't really say this is getting any easier. It is different. I have a constant hurt on the inside. I feel like I am already dead and must simply hang around. Oh Alex, will there ever be any peace in this life again? Maybe, just maybe it will be in watching your brother grow. What a wonderful young man he is.

Yesterday Morgan turned fourteen years old. We had a big party for him, and you would have been so proud of his behavior. He was gracious and kind. Like a Pied Piper, all the little kids were around him and he seemed to have a lot of fun. I hope so. I put on a public face but it really took a toll. I am so tired. I want only to sit by myself and think of you. The only person that I look forward to seeing (other than Dad and your brother) is Barbara. It is like she is the only other person that really understands what I am going through and how I feel.

A long weekend ahead of us. Don't know what to do about Memorial Day

I love you, Alex, forever.

July 11, 1994
Dear Alex,

I feel this horrible depression again. All I want to do is cry and cry and die. Alex, you were one person. Why am I feeling so terrible? As much as I love you, I love your dad and Morgan. Or do I love you more than anything? Are we specially bonded forever and is that why I cannot accept your death? When you were alive I know I loved you a lot, but I never thought I loved you more than dad and Morgan. Maybe I feel this way just because you are gone, but whatever the reason the pain does not seem to get any better. I stand over your grave and want to go down there with you. Never, ever did I think I would welcome death, and now I just want release from all this pain. I will not commit suicide but I know I am playing Russion Roulette with many things, like I am defying the world to keep me alive. Why, why, why should I have to do this? I know I'm not a saint, but I have never tried to intentionally hurt anyone and have tried to be kind. What have I done to warrant this suffering?

July 19, 1994 Children's Memorial Day for State of Oregon
Dear Alex,

I heard from you on Sunday when I was in so much pain. I felt like I was going to die on the spot from the agony of seeing you, in my mind, during the accident. Envisioning your body is so dreadful and I don't know what to do when the vision won't go away. I went into my closet, to be alone, and was holding onto your shirt. I was doubled over crying when my old jewelry-music box played two notes. That old thing has not worked in years, and I knew it was you trying to comfort me. The next morning I went in and tried to make that thing play a note and could not get a sound. I know it was you, and I am so grateful for this knowledge. Not having you here is agony, but knowing you still exist does make it easier.

I love you.

August 12, 1994
Dear Alex,

How can I go to Hawaii without you? I see you everywhere, your long and lanky body spread out and reading a book. No boredom for you. Hat on backward. I miss you so much, my son. How can we do this? Come to see me, please.

August 17, 1994
Dear Alex,

I have been thinking of you all day. I brought a lock of your hair with us to Hawaii so that in some way you can travel, also. Where do I leave it? Got so upset that I called Laurie. You seem further away here, but seeing your name and having the dream helped. I feel so selfish—other people have such hard lives and mine isn't, EXCEPT FOR THE GRIEF. I live well, eat well. We were so alike. Love to do what we want, when we want. I miss having you next to me for the hula and with me when dad and Morgie went for a hike. You would have been here with me, reading. I miss you, but it isn't as hard here as I thought it would be.

September 3, 1994
Dear Alex,

I'm so mad at you. How can I live with these visions in my head of this horrible accident? How could you leave us like that? I see you driving and laughing and screwing off and then it's all over. So fast. Your wonderful life is over and we are left to pick up and continue. I want to die instead. I haven't said, "It's not fair" very much, and I know life isn't fair, but how can this be? How can I grasp death and not ever seeing my son again? This pain is so horrible. If you can see into my mind, you know the truth of this. Why can't you help more? Am I being selfish? Are you with others trying to help them, or are you unable to do any more than you have. I know you still exist, but right now I need constant confirmation. And please don't say my faith in this belief should be enough. If I cannot touch you and hug you, I at least need to feel your presence. Oh, Alex, this is too much to ask, and yet what do I do? I am trapped with no way out. I cannot bear this pain, but I have to. How could I possibly do to Dad and Morgan what you did to us? That is how I have to look at it. Sometimes you seem so selfish, having had your fun and paid the price, yet it is we who are really paying. How could you do that?

Someone brought an apple to you at the cemetery today Alex. I actually smiled, because you hated apples, but what a sweet thing for a friend to do. Oh Alex, you had many sweet friends. Why did you leave them? Why did you leave us my baby?

There is nothing left of my insides, and my body feels like it is dying. It probably isn't, but I don't want to live without you and if my body would die on its own, then it would not be my fault. Absolutely pitiful and ridiculous, isn't it? If I let my body die, then it is the same as killing myself only slower. But I cannot help my deepest wish. I need to see you and I know if I died I would. I am afraid of death, but I guess the pain is so bad sometimes that I figure it is better than this. My little boy, whom I protected (overprotected), loved, cherished, and would give my life for, how could you leave me? How, how, how?

This is so wrong to want to die, but how do I get through this? My whole life is in front of me and I cannot face it. How does a person have a life with half her heart gone? It was ripped out of me and I don't think it will ever come back. How could you die? How? I need you to be here. Oh, Alex. Where are you? Are you happy? Can you see me? Do you feel my pain? Do you see the pain your dad and brother are in? I feel like I am going to explode. And then I feel selfish for thinking these things. My mind won't ever rest and I am so tired.

September 24, 1994
Dearest Alex,

I had a gift today. The mom of one of your friends, Sarah, wrote to tell me wonderful things about you and how much they grieve for you. Hearing these kind things and knowing you are not forgotten mean so very much to me.

I know deep in my heart I am very angry at you for leaving all of us to mourn you. Oh Alex. We miss you so much. I miss you so much. Our perfect little family is gone. Poor Morgan is left to pick up the pieces and try to fill both places.

What hurts most, besides constantly missing you is that life is moving on. We are making plans for next summer's vacation and inside I am screaming, How can this be? Right now the most important future plans take place on November 3, 1994. This is when I get to see George Anderson and have a more direct contact with you. Please don't disappoint me, Alex. Your dad is worried that I will be crushed and he is right. I need to know you are alright and are with me at least some of the time. Please be with me Alex.

October 9, 1994
Dearest Alexander,

You sent two nice ladies to me at the cemetery this morning. Strangers, who came to comfort me. Thank you, Son.

I have such emptiness in me. Oh Alex, there are days that I don't think this is worth it. I don't want to be here doing these worthless deeds—nothing seems important, except Morgan and your father. Should we give everything up and start over, find what is important? Will anything ever be again?

I'm not sleeping again, or at least not very well. Please Alex, you are responsible for this horror in my life—please, please, help me sleep. Either visit me in my dreams or send sweet dreams for me to get rest. I know I am not capable of doing this without sleep. I know that maybe I'm not doing great even with sleep, but it is the best I am capable of right now. Without sleep, I am capable of nothing. I just want to curl into a ball and make the world go away.

Will I ever get the pictures of the accident out of my mind? I keep trying to fix it. Did Brett grab the wheel? Why wasn't he wearing a seat belt? Why were you going so fast? Why did you have to die? I don't want it to be you that is gone. When I think of it, I am horrified and can hardly breathe. How can I continue without you? Dammit, Alex, how could you do this to all of us. We love you and need you here. I go between being so angry with you and wanting to hold you so badly. My heart is gone and you took it away. How could you?

November 23, 1994
Dear Alex,

It has been so long since I have written and so much has happened. I did go to Alabama to see George Anderson and make contact with you and the experience was wonderful. The people, the reading with George, Raymond, and his wife Cheryl—everything by far exceeded my expectations. The following weekend I went to Seattle with a group of twelve to see George on a local TV show He saw me and Patricia outside before the show and invited us in with him, but we declined because we were with several other people. He then said he had something to send me in the mail. So I am flattered, anxious, and overwhelmed, but mostly grateful that I touched him in some way also. What a truly wonderful man.

Today is particularly hard. Until one hour ago, I hadn't heard from Cindi, Kathy, my mother, or John's mother about Thanksgiving. Kathy phoned an hour ago and left us a message wishing us "Happy Thanksgiving," but no invitation for dinner and no concern about Morgan or how tough this will be for us. I feel so bitter and angry. I know this isn't the right way, but I don't seem to be able to let it go. I want these people to leave my life. How can we get through this grief when they keep adding to it? I know I need to pray for guidance and to finally be grateful for what I do have: John, Morgan many dear friends. Are you gone because I haven't been grateful enough over the years? I remember myself crying on more than one Thanksgiving, because no family came around. But I had my family and that wasn't good enough. I know it doesn't work like that, but I feel like I am being punished and I don't even know why. Why, Why—What have I done?

January 27, 1995

A new year and this is the first time I have written in a long time. We went to Aunt Val's for Christmas and it went okay. They did not make a big production about the holiday and it was nice to be with them. I found the New Year to be even harder than other holidays. How could you never see 1995? But of course you really do see it, just from a different perspective. I know this, but it just doesn't help much when I am missing you.

January has been such a horrible month. Your 18th birthday has hung over us like doom. How could you not be here for it? There were many of your friends at the cemetery on the 21st. We held a little memorial service for you. I made brownies. We had a balloon release. I did have 50 of them, but 25 got loose, leaving only 25, exactly the amount we needed. Isn't that something? Were you helping out Alex? Larry Pettersen was there and Brett and David. I'm sure you know what bad shape they are in. Andy and Jason were there. Aunt Kathy came by. Do you know how angry I am with this family of mine and do you realize the final rift that your death caused. Do you know the pain you have left behind? I am so angry with everyone, Alex. I am mad at you. I am mad at people for not trying to help out more (emotionally). A phone call from many of them would be nice. Am I being petty with all these people? Shouldn't I be more grateful for all the people that are here and trying to help. So many kids crying and talking and remembering. How could you leave us all in this pain? Do you know I was at the tree today and died all over again? I want to feel what you felt. I want to die. I am so trapped. I cannot leave Morgan and Dad, but I need to see you. Someday is too far away. Why don't you come to me? I know you can do it. I feel much of the time like I am going to lose my mind. Alex, Alex, Alex—just letters on a page. I need to touch you and hold you, my baby. Can't you help heal my soul? If I have to stay, can't you help me.

February 14, 1995—Valentine's Day
Dear Alex,

One year ago today you bought a last gift for me, a wonderful, fun card, and a box of chocolate covered cherries. I had to wait a couple of days to eat the cherries because I had been sick, but the card made me laugh. You made a special trip to the store to get this for me, and I will always be grateful. I miss you so much and feel this weight re-descend on me as I write to you and I know I try to hide from these feelings, but think I am making progress. My heart has not been as heavy this last week, and I feel guilty about it, but also it is a nice respite from all the horrible pain. I am sure this is not over by any means, but the break is rejuvenating. It is also a time that Morgan and I are, once again, growing closer. I felt a wave of love for him the other evening. Were you watching? It was fun to play with him and laugh with your dad. Maybe I am slightly coming back to life. It has been one month short of a year since you left and I can't believe it. So long since I held you.

April 23, 1995
Dear Alex,

So much has happened; The one-year anniversary of your death. Many people remembered and yet it didn't make any difference. I went to the cemetery that night and played Tears in Heaven by Eric Clapton and lit a candle. I left the candle to burn all night long and no one put it out. It helped when I drove away to see it glowing in the dark.

I'm sure you know about the article that I wrote for the paper. So much response, and yet I know you know what I feel, a certain amount of gratification, but mostly it doesn't make a difference. I wrote the piece for myself and everything else just happened.

Last week some nuts blew up a building in Oklahoma City. So many people killed, so many children. I really really hope there is a plan in a higher place, because otherwise what would living be all about? All this pain.

September 23, 1995

I can't believe it has been so long since I have written. For some reason I have fought it. So much to share in articles and with my friends on the internet. I will list what has happened since I last wrote:

First there was the Class of '95 Awards Night. I gave out the scholarship in your name for $1000 to your friend Kelly. You know the words I said. He was wonderful and a great comfort.

Two days before graduation, which we did attend, The Oregonian did an article about you and our family. You saved us perfect seats at the ceremony; I know it was you. The procession led right to our seats and to me. (Valarie was with your dad and I.) Your buddies, Kelly & Michael stopped the line to give me a hug. Many other people gave hugs, pats, etc. Yes, some did turn away, but it doesn't really matter anymore.

Some of your friends went to the accident tree and left you a message for happiness in Spanish, in black marker on the bark. We all miss you so much. How could you leave?

Your brother started at Tualatin High. He seems very happy. Your dad and I are ripped to shreds as we have to face your school, constantly.

My small group of eight friends are getting closer. Retreat in one week.

Your locker has been taken down at the school. I was so upset and felt betrayed. They put up a blooming crab apple tree and a plaque in your honor. You are not forgotten, but it is not enough. Nothing ever will be.

The Compassionate Friends Conference: You were there and created many small miracles.

Your dad is waiting for me. I must go. Help me, Alex. Help me.

Mom

January 5, 1996

Dear Alex,

It is a new year and I am doing better. Yet, as I write those words I feel a heaviness. As I help people along, I feel better, and then I suffer because I don't want to feel better. You told me I would be a help to many and I appear to be, but I don't want to become self-important. I am no different than others, but my grief is personal to me. I don't cry often anymore, but the tears are there, just frozen inside.

Life has totally moved on for many and also for me. I closed my business and relish the decision. It really was no longer for me. I plan on writing a book in honor of you, but also to educate about grief. The grief process is made so much harder by the clueless. Do you know about the The Compassionate Friends newsletter? I am the editor. Can you believe it? Many people are very kind and gracious and make me feel as if I am doing a very special thing and have a special gift. Mostly it has been a huge gift to me and helped me with my grief. Two people from TCF want to start helping and I was feeling very much an ownership about doing it. But they each lost a child, too, and I really could use the help and besides, it is their group and newsletter, also.

We went to the Ogle's house again for Christmas and it was okay.

Have I told you how hard it is to look at your picture? Waves of disbelief still rush over me. I will never understand how you can be dead and I am alive. I realized the other day that I have worried about you your whole life, worried that something would happen to you, and it did. There wasn't anything I could do, was there? But I keep trying to fix it and I just can't.

This year for Christmas I put a wreath at the cemetery and a wreath at the tree. We also bought another cemetery plot and put a tree and plaque up on it. I do, do, do and it doesn't make any difference because you are still gone.

Darren came to visit you at the cemetery over Christmas. He left you a gift and a note. Joyce went with me to visit you and helped me mourn and Susan also went one day—you know Drew don't you.

I love you Alex. My love for you, and I think your love for me, is what is nurturing me.

Mom

January 13, 1996
Dear Alex,

Tomorrow I leave for LA with several friends. We will all be meeting with George Anderson. For me, the second time. I have really mixed feelings because I know this will not bring you back, but I so need to hear from you.

Wednesday was an awful day of grief. Days like those take me right back to the moment that I was told that my beautiful Alex was dead, never to be held again. I still can't grasp that in my brain, Alex. It seems so very cruel, and so much of me is angry with you for letting me down and causing this horrible pain. I've had a lot of pain in my life and I resent more. I can't believe that we are approaching your 19th birthday and the second date of your death. Where have these two years gone?

Please, please son send me a message of hope and strength wrapped in something I will recognize from you. I love you and for you I have chosen to stay, not because I do not believe that I wouldn't be with you if I took my own life..but I do know that suicide is not the way.

Talk to you on Monday. Please bring the others with you, particularly Brad.

Love,
Mom

February 4, 1996
Dear Alex,

I know I don't need to tell you what transpired at the meeting with George, plus I have it all on tape for my own memory, but I need to talk about how I am now. I am melancholy. What an old-fashioned word, but it seems to fit. I am so sad all the time, and yet I am resolved to move forward. Your scolding helped to a degree, but I think it is easier, from where you sit, to understand. You are my son, and being lectured by you on life when you left this life through your own will is difficult. I know I resent it. But thank you for telling me about your frame of mind and your health problem.

While it breaks my heart to have confirmed that your hyperactivity was truly the cause of your behavior that led to your death, at the same time I now realize that this was really beyond your control. You weren't just being defiant and irresponsible. My God, how can this be?

I am afraid that I am getting mean because of this anger in me about your leaving. I struck out at a not-very-nice man who is in grief over his cat. I think this is being petty on my part, but I don't feel petty. I feel hurt that someone thinks a cat's death is on par with yours or all the other children that died. I want him to understand the life-altering event of your death. I am sure his life is not altered. But am I being too judgmental? I am very confused and afraid.

While I don't really think he has a clue, he really wasn't hurting me and yet I felt compelled to strike out. I do know that I should apologize, but in this instance (and probably others) I just can't find it in me.

You have to know my fears about your brother. I know you said not to smother, but how do I refrain from protecting him? Where is that fine line? If only he could understand the difference between being appropriately protective and overly protective. I am so afraid of something happening to him. I am in a hurry for him to grow up, so that I can quit being afraid, but I also know that it probably won't make a difference. I will always fear for his life.

I'm tired of all of this, Alex.

You know I love you and also what is in my heart,

Mom

February 13, 1996

Dear Alex,

What an awful morning this has been. I am so sad and depressed. I feel my life is totally out of my control and am so very tired of fighting. My clothes are so terribly tight and I am uncomfortable. I want to feel better, but feel unable to take the action necessary. Why is this?

When did I become so weak-willed? Everything is tinged with pain. Oh, Alex, you have so many answers, Why? I know you told me that it was your time, but why anyway. Why? I can't stand this pain. I feel helpless and hopeless.

Where do I start? I am so overwhelmed.

Mom

March 10, 1996...Sunday

Dear Alex,

You knew that Brad's father, and our friend, Leo, was going to die. He went on February 26. This has thrown my life into a tailspin again. It seems like I had found a kind of life that I was functioning in, and then it was all swept away by this. Leo is with his Brad and my Alex. He has the answers. He can hold his son. Why Leo? I wanted to go so badly and so did Brad's mom, Barb, so why Leo? My mind has trouble grasping that he is gone.

Do you know the spiritual trauma this has caused? Just when I think I might have something kind of figured out this happened. Is there a God? If you exist, my Alex, then there has to be a God and you do exist. You have to, otherwise nothing means anything. How can I have faith? What do I do? I have searched and listened and judged and tried. What is the answer? Have you deserted me? Am I living too much for you? So much of me was killed with you, Alex. You are only one person and must not have all of the answers. Why is it so impossible for you to contact me in a way that makes me know? For me, knowing would make all of the difference. Then I wouldn't care what anyone else said or thought. Why is that so wrong to want? Life has not been a picnic and then you left anyway. I need you in my life.

I am not suicidal anymore, but so much of me still wishes to die so that I can know and see and touch you. Even knowing the pain this would cause so many people, I can't help wanting to be with you. This life feels so burdened. I worry all the time and I feel worthless. I know in my mind that people care and that I am worthwhile, but in my heart and emotions I don't think I will ever believe it.

Here I am crying and feeling sorry for myself again. This is such a helpless feeling. It will be two years this coming Friday since you died. How could you go and die? I have asked you that a thousand times. How many more times will I ask it until I get an answer? Or have you answered and I am just too hurt and stubborn to listen. This is too hard and I don't want to do it. It is easy from there to pick a path, but from here it hurts too badly. Why would this much pain be good?

So many people have lost children and there is so much pain. These questions haunt me and I don't know what to do. Help me, Alex. I know you can. I will try to listen for the answer.

I love you more than my life,

Mom

April 7, 1996

Dear Alex,

So many thoughts swirling in my head. I just finished a book by Melodie Beattie about grief and moving forward. She wrote my thoughts and so much of my path. I have been so dead and continue to struggle to see beyond the gray. I laugh but don't mean it (always with an edge of hysteria). I cry, but resent it because I am tired of crying; I hurt, but am learning to live with this pain (unless I dig at the scab). What does my future hold? I still resist the thought of a future at all.

I am very focused on Morgan, but that frightens me. Of course, you know what happened last night. He fell asleep on the floor and when I went to awaken him I noticed how much he resembled you and yet he was in such a deep sleep (on his back) that he reminded me of you in the casket. I was terrified and started shaking him awake. I am so afraid of tomorrow with the fear of losing Morgan or Dad. How can a person function and move on in this fear? I try not to think about it, but it is pervasive. It crawls up my throat like it is alive and I can hardly breathe.

I have to find a focus or I will never move beyond fear and self-torture and self-pity. Help me Alex.

My birthday was Wednesday and you sent two gifts. The medium James Van Praagh and a special dream. Thank you, Alex for the people in my life, especially Barbara and her gift of love. Thank you for Susan and so many others. They all help.

We went to the Stanley's for Easter dinner and had a pleasant time. It is easy to be with them. I am grateful for their friendship. I got a nice hug from Aaron. He reminds me a lot of you.

Thanks for trying to ease my pain. I will continue to try, but please remember the only thing that will truly, truly help is for me to see you. I know you can do this Alex. Brad, Leo, and my small group will help. Please son. Help me so that I can help others. I love you my sweet boy and am trying not to become bitter when I realize you aren't here.

Mom

April 8, 1996
Dear Alex,

I am going to try to write daily about my thoughts and experiences. Maybe it will truly help me find the way. I spent the largest portion of this day alone and it was okay. Did some work on the newsletter and babied my back some.

Went to book club and it was alright, but I always feel like such a fake, making nice and being funny and not feeling any of it. The women are truly nice people, but they have happy lives, and I feel so separate, except for Susan. Certainly I feel close to Fredda and Laurie, but during the book club I feel disconnected. It is really strange because I realize that I can be funny and that I tend to lead the group, but I resent it and feel like I am not really there. I am not sure why I stay in. Maybe a feeling of responsibility that if I leave the group will disband. I helped start it and feel responsible and it is the only thing I do not revolving around grief. While right now it is not fun, maybe someday it will be.

Have been having trouble going to sleep lately, so am staying up really late and sleeping in late. This is not a great pattern.

Talked to Tigard High about speaking at the driving assembly and am waiting to hear if it will work out. Why do I want this? Honestly, I believe I need to be out there with my pain, to get through the thick skulls of these kids and save their lives and to have your life validated and recognized.

Tomorrow I will attempt to meditate. Visit me soon.

I love you, Alex.

Mom

April 11, 1996

Dear Alex,

Another long and slow and painful day. Was in your room going through things and was overwhelmed with the loss of you. Will I ever feel anything peaceful or happy again? I don't think so. Morgan makes me a little happy but no peace. I worry non-stop about his safety and happiness. I was thinking today that just being dead would be so nice. No worries, no pain and I could watch over Morgan like a guardian angel. Is that what Leo is doing? It seems so cruel. How could you leave us Leo, and if you had to, why aren't you showing up to help us. I'm so mad at you. Where are you? Bring the kids and come to visit. Let us know. Let us know.

I want to die. I don't want to cause pain to others and I don't want to kill myself, but I want to die. I feel heavy in my heart and body, lethargic like I don't want to do anything, afraid of what the future holds. Why, God, Why. Why let me live and take my son. I want to go, but I can't bear to bring pain to John and Morgan. I am so trapped. Dear Lord, what do I do? How do I continue to survive when it feels like it is getting harder? I am 43 years old. Hasn't there been enough?

Mom

April 26, 1996

Dear Alex,

About two weeks ago I woke up and felt better and had a respite from overwhelming grief and despair for awhile. Today I woke up and all the heaviness was back. I have been very tired this week and despondent I took some news about the TCF newsletter badly and mostly feel that there is no point to anything, anymore. Then I look into your brother's eyes and I know the point. But I am so very tired, Alex. I don't know where to go from here.

I love you,
Mom

April 28, 1996
Dear Alex,

It is very late, about 11:30 P.M. on a Sunday night. Been a very quiet day with your brother and your dad. Went to visit you at the cemetery by myself and trimmed your grave. Audel's mom stopped by for a minute.

Got our young big-foot a new pair of size 15 shoes and then came home.took a nap, cooked a nice dinner and watched some TV. I have felt a creeping heaviness in my throat all day. Kind of a despondency, and an unspoken grief. A day like today seems worthless. What is life really about? My mind is all a muddle.

I am worried about Daddy. He isn't well. Morgan and I cannot bear to lose dad. We will be lost too. Both of us have had enough for this lifetime. However it works, Dad and I must stay for the duration. The aloneness would be too much to bear.

I creep around this house by myself on many days. Why don't I see you? With all the help available, why can't you come to me? Am I asking too much? I just don't believe it. Many, many people see their loved ones after passing on. If they can, you can. You are my son and made of the stuff to succeed. If I can survive your death and reinvest in life, then the least you can do is come around. I know I am a bossy mother. But what else can I say? I feel so terribly helpless. You know my heart, Alex. Get past the difficulties and come to my aid before I lose my mind, because some days I feel so close.

Enough lecturing. You could try lecturing back. An open discussion in my dreams would be a good place to start.

Because of my love for you, I have chosen to stay on this earth. Please help it be a little easier.

Mom

May 3, 1996
Dear Alex,

This week I worked really hard on a speech that I gave at a MADD program at Tigard High. I was so nervous and upset, honey. My stomach carried on and I was sick, but I did it, and it went well. I believe that I really touched these kids, many who knew you. Several introduced themselves, some were your friends' younger siblings or some knew you in grade school, and others were just concerned. I was proud of them and of myself.

This has brought up a lot of stuff about the accident, though. I woke up crying and thoughts of losing my mind, again. I hope that this won't be a consistent pattern. I would like to talk to young people. Very selfishly I love to talk about you and the talking helps me express my grief, but it also helps others. We'll see.

May 4, 1996
Dear Alex,

It is mid-afternoon on a Saturday and I feel so heavy hearted. There is a huge lump in my throat and I am on the verge of tears. I know this is loneliness. Morgan went with a friend's family to a BBQ and that is wonderful for him, but I miss him when he is gone. And I am envious that he is at a family function when that just isn't in our future. I feel very alone in the world even though I have your dad and Morgan. Why is this?. I am feeling lost.

May 12, 1996
Dear Alex,

It's that day again. My third Mother's Day without you. I am doing okay. Doing a lot of thinking and reading. *Conversations with God*, is quite a book and has given me a lot of food for thought. It really seems to be helping me at some level.

I know I need to get past this self hate and this constant whipping of myself for I don't even know what. I do want to be more like you and not carry petty jealousy and hurt feelings because I am not, or I feel I am not, included. I want to ask how to accomplish this, but I know the answer. Mostly I want it to be time to come home and be with you and my grandma and my dad. Reconciling myself is one thing, but truly wishing to stay is another.

Morgan and I seem to be getting very close. You must be watching over him. He is so beautiful and full of fun and playfulnessand he has a lot of your qualities. His singing continues to give me such joy.

I am feeling sorry for myself these last few days about my family. I do believe that they are on the path they need to be, but I don't know how to get past the hurt and resentment. Because I can't fool you or myself, I want them to hurt for hurting me and I know I need to get past it. Life is moving on without you, but I know you feel my pain every-day and no time truly goes by that I don't think of you. I want to hold you in my arms so badly. I miss you.

Love,
Mom

May 27, 1996—Memorial Day & Morgan's 16th birthday
Dear Alex,

I guess the above line says it all. Can you believe that Morgan is 16? It seems like yesterday when it was you. I also can't believe that his birthday falls on Memorial Day this year. I can't be unhappy because of his birthday, but I can't be happy because it is my day of remem-brance for you, mostly, and Grandma and my dad. Caught in the mid-dle with my emotions right in my throat. I waver between tears, anger, and emotional paralysis and am trying to keep it all bottled up and hid-den from Morgan.

I thought I wanted to write, but really don't. Help me through tomor-row and send a special something for your brother. I love you, sweetheart.
Mom

June 16, 1996—Father's Day
Dear Alex,

I am in a very depressed mood and am filled with tears. How did this happen again? I know it is the anger with you, Alex. How am I ever going to let this go? I am kind of excited about seeing the medium, James, but that is getting to be an old story. Will you talk to me and will you say what I need to hear? I hope you know what that is, because I sure don't. Have I become a psychic chaser like others I know of? They haven't found happiness and neither have I.

What is going to happen now Alex? My patience is strung out, my anger is raw, my wish to leave here is strong. This earth is so horrible and I am sick of all the brutality, pain, hate, anguish, and my own self-hate. Why can't I quit hating myself so much. I regret the kind of mother I was to you. I learned how to be a mother through parenting you and it's not fair. I want to go back and erase all the mistakes. I want to give you more freedom. I feel so betrayed by you, Alex. How could you leave? You left a mess for us to clean up and our own broken hearts to try and mend.

I am filled with all these feelings of incompleteness, frustration, hurt, and disappointment in people. How do I draw people into my life that will hurt me? Where does it end? I want it to end. I want it to end. I want it to end. Your dad has the right idea, trust nobody, ever, ever, ever.

June 18, 1996
Dear Alex,

Had my therapy group and TCF meeting tonight. Both great learning experiences. I don't know what to do about group and about leaving TCF. I feel ready in some areas and not in others, but my instinct says it is time to go. I am unclear.

I'm also very tired, but wanted to make note that tonight was my first time to facilitate a sharing group at TCF. It went well and I feel that I did a decent job. Were you with me Alex? I'm yawning and guess it is bedtime. I did feel some anguish on the way home, Alex. I still don't believe it. I love you. It has been a long time since I held you. Please come to me tonight and help me remember.

Mom

July 20, 1996
Dear Alex,

Went to TCF Conference in Long Beach, California. Met with James Van Praagh and had a group reading. Felt that I truly spoke with you. Next time we talk I would like to hear more, so much more, on how you feel about your life when it was here, with us. Do you see your brother and Daddy? This is so important.

Have you been helping me decipher these feelings about group and TCF newsletter? You know I reached the decision to leave both and feel the decision is for good reasons. I do not like the leadership position in TCF and much prefer facilitating. I feel strong enough to leave group.

I am scattered tonight and feel that you are very far away. Is this how it is going to be for the rest of my life? I am numb inside. I still need you to stay close, yet I feel greedy and selfish for continuing to ask. If you tell me to let you go, tell me how to do it. There is no other you and it is so easy to get overwhelmed with loss.

I love you.
Mom

July 28, 1996
Dear Son,

I went to see you at the cemetery tonight. I still can't believe I am standing at the grave of my son. How can this be?

Have you been sending people to me lately? Both Cheryl & Dianne think I should write. How do I go about this and what should I write about Alex. You, grief, what? I don't know where to start, but when I do a letter or produce the newsletter, I feel satisfaction. Is this my path? I wish you could just tell me if I am on the right track or I am looking for acclaim and ways to keep busy so that I don't have to try at meditation and being still with myself? Will that come in time? I know I am working hard, but where am I going. Will I work this hard and then just die? Is that what I am supposed to do?

You probably know me better than I know me, but maybe not. I do know that I want to be very public about my grief and you. Good night sweetheart.

I love you.

Momma

September 26, 1996

Dear Alex,

I feel like a big pile of nothing but grief, tears, questions, and anxiety. Will it ever end? How could you do this to me?

October 20, 1996

Dear Alex,

I don't know how much better things are. It got really bad for awhile. My last entry was the beginning of a downward spiral, which culminated last Monday into a day of despair, a wish to die, and constant and continual tears. I don't ever want to go through a time like that again. The pain was so terrible.

I miss you, Alex. I don't sense your presense and then I doubt your continued existence. When I doubt your existence I can't bear it. Thank goodness for Morgan and for Dad. They are the only reasons that I stay. I may be failing some test in life, but so be it. I do think of what other people are experiencing, and I try not to feel so sorry for myself, but I tend to jump either one way or another. I am far too judgemental about myself and this all-consuming grief I have for you, or I wallow in a pit of despair and can't find a way out.

You have the answers and I guess I'm really mad at you for not helping more. Maybe nothing you could do would ever be enough, but hearing about the wonders of heaven doesn't really help. I've always know you were okay, but what about us. Our connection was special, but I still feel that you betrayed me and my trust. I wish I could talk with you so you could explain yourself and even say I'm sorry. Are you sorry, Alex? Despite what was supposed to be, are you sorry? We are so very hurt, so many of us.

I need to hear your voice, at the very least in my dreams; I need to hold you. Where are you, Alex? Where are you? Please help me and send my grandma. I need help.

Dear Alex,
I am pasting in a letter that I sent to Aunt Val. Pretty much sums up tonight.

Dear Val,

I knew I shouldn't do it, but I did anyway and am now paying the price. I watched a show called ER. Unfortunately tonight the main thrust was about a car accident. While I taped the show and could fast-forward through a lot of it, there is no way to fast forward through the emotions it brought up. I usually like the show, but have to be very careful about when I watch it. Nights are bad. I can't sleep and pictures are running through my head, pictures that never truly leave, but that I don't look at very much anymore. It makes all the raw agony come screaming back up to the front. Then I miss him more, more than I can bear. When I feel like this I don't know where to turn or what to do, because nobody can make it better. Nobody can say anything that really helps. I just have to feel it and feel it until the rawness subsides and goes back to being an oozing wound that just hurts constantly. I don't know how I get through some days.

I would have called you tonight, but it was too late. Maybe it was all for the best anyway. No one needs this kind of call. In fact, I don't really make these pain calls anymore, but tonight it hit hard. I wish the world would stop so that I could step off and take a break.

November 12, 1996
Dear Alex,
All day, so depressed that I can barely get out of bed. Hiding it from everyone. Don't know where to turn or what to do. Like a huge heavy weight pushing in on me and I feel like I am going mad.

Why do I feel like my life is truly over? I have no goals or ambitions. I don't feel as if my friends really understand or even care anymore. I want to go away and be with you where there is no pain and no worry. I'm so tired of it all Alex. I don't want to work this hard. What do I do next?

January 10, 1997
Dear Alex,

What a couple of months it has been. Once again I made it through the holidays, but they were rugged.

You know, of course, about my current plight with the pinched nerve in my back and the cyst in my breast. These have both given me pause to really think and reach a decision. I have decided to live, to really live. As much as I want to see you, all I can see is the pain it would cause your dad and brother if I let myself die. So while I may have brought this on myself, in an effort to let my body die, I no longer need it. Or maybe this is a swift kick in the butt from you. Whatever the case, I will go toward a future. I can't really let myself think about what this means, planning a future without you in it, but I will take it one day at a time. I will take good care of your brother and daddy, and finally, I promise to take care of myself.

I love you so much, my beautiful son, who knew me so well, could read my mind. I can get crazy when I think about life without you, but I will no longer dwell on this. I love you and I will try not to fall into despair as your 20th birthday approaches.

But, please don't leave me yet. I am not ready to let you go totally. Please stay with me, son. I still need to hear from you.

Mom

November 15, 1997
Dear Alex,

You didn't let me down, but I didn't really expect you to show up. Of course, I mean James Van Praague's seminar. During the course of the evening, I asked a question and he told me that my son was standing behind my right shoulder, I felt you. You touched me and I felt waves of electricity shoot through me. As this continued through the night I felt that this was your way of comforting me because you wouldn't come through. It is funny because it would have been alright. My need for this kind of intervention has diminished and I hoped many other children would come throught to their parents.

When James asked permission to come to me I was flabbergasted. I wish I could remember everything he said. He talked about the tree we planted for you at the cemetery, the picture I look at of you, that I have started to write a book about you,and most important, that when I write you stand behind me (Are you there now?) I think I can feel you. It's like a thickness in my throat and stomach and a heady feeling. You told everyone about my bad knees—so much like you; about my stomach problems and that I would lose the weight that I have put on since losing you; about my sitting on your bed and crying and holding your things; about my having kept everything that belonged to you; about the bicycle discussions with Dad and Morgan. James told me daddy's name and asked who John was. You sent love to Dad. He said Daddy is still in much pain. He talked about your death and how sudden it was. He said he liked you and you were growing up. I know this from when I see you for a visit in my dreams. Is this one of the ways you will help me over this mountain. He also said something about collecting but I didn't know what that was—maybe dad's baseball card collection.

Alex, it does help to know that you are with me. Maybe as I struggle through this depression and I know you are here, that very knowledge will help me. I will try and take better care of myself.

Thank you, Alex. You never let me down. Help Daddy and Morgan. (I'm sure you are.)

I love you,
Momma

November 24, 1997
Dear Alex,

I have really been sick this last week. And of course spending too much time in my head. Is that what you learned on this earth, how to not always be in your head, but to feel? I look back at your life, Alex, and am learning now how to do it right. Maybe your hyperactivity was your way of being free from conventions and learning about compassion, being on the side no one wants to be on. I know you didn't love everybody and that forgiving each person who hurt you was difficult, but I also know that if these people would have offered you a true apology, honestly wanting to be your friend, you would forgive them.

You have a huge heart and so much compassion. I am so proud of you. I know you are still like that because you are taking so much time with me. I'm sorry that you are still so manacled to my emotions, but I also know that you understand. Don't you honey? I miss you so. Every relationship is so special and unique, and so was ours. We seemed to be in sync so much. I miss that easy camaraderie with my child, with you.

I know that I am also suffering from this overriding depression. Can you help? Drugs do not seem to be the answer for me. (I think I just caught a thought from you that helping others will help me.) I do know this, but how can I when I can't move from the chair? I feel trapped. Send me what help and prayers and energy you can, and I will try harder.

Remember, the holidays are their own kind of hell. I am sorry to feel that way, but I do. Maybe it will be easier this year with my sisters back. But Alex, they are not you. Nobody can fill that empty space.

I am trying to avoid doing things for personal recognition, because it feels wrong. But I also realize that sometimes I search this out thinking that it will fill that empty space. It doesn't. I still don't know my direction. It is funny, people keep saying I will write a book and be on Oprah and you know that I find that appealing. I want the world to see you and recognize my grief and to have the pain of all grievers validated in this world. I still get so angry with the people that just want it all to go away because they do not want to be inconvenieced by emotion.

I need to go to bed. I love you. I will see you.

Love,

Mom

January 20, 1998

My darling boy, Alex,

Today is your 21st birthday. I think you are celebrating it in heaven, even though the day was mostly pain for Dad and me. Did you pop in and see us light the candles and tell the stories? Christina was here. She walked all the way from Texaco carrying two plants, a purple one for you and another plant for me. She can't even afford those. What a true friend she was to you and has become to us. She took the day off of work and offered to spend the whole day with us. What a sweet girl. I did take her home to Portland tonight.

Joyce and Doug were here, too. I didn't call them until around 1:00 P.M. to invite them and Joyce had already done dinner for that night. They put that aside and came to be with us. This means so much to me. Your birthday was remembered by Aunt Kathy, Kirsti, Aunt Val, Mary Fribley, Carol, Susan. We received a card from Brad & Jana in your honor.

Daddy found the beautiful rose poster that you gave to me several years ago. It had gotten pretty beat up, but we took it to the frame shop anyway and cut the edges down and framed it in a green frame. It looks absolutely beautiful hanging in our bedroom. The rest of the day I worked on a collage of pictures of you and Morgan for frames I bought.

I've spent a lot of the last few days crying and having this heavy feeling inside. It does feel as if it has been forever since I've seen you. I feel defeated, as if I thought that I would succeed and this would end and I am now realizing that this will only end when I die and get to see you again. I will always carry this sadness. My precious son, you were so kind and never did a cruel thing to anyone. Why did you do this unthinking thing to your family? I am trying to hard to let go of the resentment and I will continue to try. Help me.

I wrote a story as a gift to you for your 21st birthday, called Wake Up, My Son. I know you can hear the words in my heart. Happy Birthday, Alex.

I love you.

July 25, 1998
Dear Alex,

Very trying times. Just when I think there is a little light ahead then another challenge presents itself. I am tired of that word challenge and I am tired of the challenges. I want some peace and the ability to make the search and find the meaning without any more trauma.

I am so worried about Morgan that it has become an obsession. What will happen to him? I know that my test is to let him go. Easier said than done.

These words sound so logical and well thought out, but do they ever show the agony of helplessness and despair. This morning I thought, *I want to die.* I am so weary of the fight and can't imagine any reward on the other side to be great enough to have to endure this constant pain of the heart.

Can you not give any hope to me? Morgan doesn't believe you still exist. Why can't you show him in some way? He needs hope too. Where have you been for me? I feel deserted and punished and I don't care that patience is a virtue. Where are you and why can't I feel you?

(The computer just went down and I lost several paragraphs. Maybe it is a way of telling me that those lost words shouldn't be said, so I will not re-say them).

I haven't been to the cemetery to see you in over six weeks. I don't think I have ever gone that long before. I am feeling the pull.

Please come to me—show me that you are near. Help your brother find his way. Please Alex.

Love,
Mom

July 31, 1998
Dear Alex,

I am starting a new diary on my new computer. As I write this I am remembering that my Mac computer was new when you died. Life is moving on and it makes me so sad.

Thank you, my son for helping me the last couple of days. I know that you, with the help of God, have answered my prayers. I asked for help to calm down, bring my blood pressure down, and let me know you are there. You did all this, and then I received a note from a friend of yours right before my oral surgery. The note just said that they think of you often and still go to the cemetery to visit you. I'm sure it was a girl because of a smiley face on the bottom. It was signed, "a friend." This meant so much to me and I know it isn't a coincidence. You helped. I feel better. I love you.

Things have eased up around here just this last two days. Morgan and I, however, have not been doing well, arguing all the time, dirty looks from him, and me walking on egg shells. This is all new territory for us, Alex. You never got to be 18 and have this much freedom. My heart still hurts over that but Mo has reached 18 and is really feeling and testing his tether. I am trying to let go and I am sure you see this. Besides losing you and Mo's illness as a baby, this is one of the hardest times I have ever gone through.

Beside that (and if I can get my health back) I think things are OK. I feel very close to your dad. We spend a lot of time together and in many ways are closer than ever. We have good friends together and apart. I am blessed with many really close friends that each offer something different for my life. I am learning the lessons of what I think my life path is, most of them the hard way, but I am finally getting it. My next big goal is to get past this lesson of physical pain. I am really tired of it, but the other night I did use the tool that Lina, my spiritual counselor, gave me, remembering that pain is just a sensation. It did help.

Please keep showing up: I would prefer having a dream where I can hold you, but I do hang onto the other signs. There is still a part of me that feels I am being punished and that you will only come if I do 'it' right. I'm working on it.

Love,
Mom

August 1, 1998
Dear Alex,

I am feeling better tonight. I had oral surgery last night and the last 18 hours have been painful. Not unbearable, but not great. This afternoon about 4:00 it started to feel a lot better and I am grateful. The swelling is also going down.

Dropped by to see Mo at work tonight. He waited on us let us tease him and have a little fun, and he seemed to enjoy it. I think we have passed our crisis for whatever reason. Did you help him, Alex, or did this just play out the way it needed to? He needs to know that you are around. We all do. Goodnight.

I love you,
Mom

August 21, 1998
Dear Alex,

Today is a Friday and I woke up in depression. I believe it has been creeping up on me for a few days, but I have been ignoring it. I guess it has reached the point where I can no longer ignore it.

I've been thinking a lot about you lately. Of course, I always think about you but I have learned how not to keep you at the forefront of my mind. The last few days, though, you are right there, and I feel such sadness. I have finally figured out that part of the reason is that it is Morgan's senior year of high school. You never got one. If you were here this would be your senior year in college and you would be close to graduation. Of course, there is no guarantee that you would have gone to college or even finished, but this is how we think it would have gone. So we are preparing for Morgan to graduate and you never will.

I feel so terribly overwhelmed with grief and wonder what the point is of my existence when I feel like a failure as a mother. I know that I tried my best, but it doesn't seem good enough and there are no replays. How could things have gone so terribly wrong with my life? Regardless of what my spiritual belief in the hereafter is, it is really hard to keep going.

I am spending most of today alone and can maybe get a handle on things for awhile. My stomach hurts, I am tired and just want to crawl into bed. Obviously, I have a few things to deal with.

I love you.
Ma

September 13, 1998

It is almost 3:00A.M. and I cannot get to sleep. I am writing the book in my head and thinking about a nice email I got from my friend Dianne, praising the the work I have done on the book. I found this to be a bit exciting and definitely mind motivating.

The bad thing, though, is I am going back to the night of the day you died. I hate doing this. It no longer is something I want to do, but it creeps up on me. How can this be good for me now? I toss and turn; cry and think and try to fix it. My mind darts and I keep begging you to come and see me in my dreams. Sometimes I feel so alone; those times are mostly when you brother turns away.

I know he is just being his age, but it continues to hurt my feelings when he pulls away and gets mad. Then I just want to ice up towards him, but I know that would be wrong. I am really tired of having my emotions pulled, trounced on, manipulated. I go through this about you and then I let him do it to me, also. I am trying hard to hang on to me and make a new life, but sometimes it just seems impossible.

I will write the book and I know it will be good. I want to do well and talk about you and this debilitating grief. There, I said it and it makes me feel sad. I don't want any gain from your death, but I guess I want recognition for surviving it, and I want the world to know that we bereaved parents, do not get over it. Not ever! You are not a disease to recover from. Please come to me tonight and once again help me through this rough patch of sadness.

I love you.

Mom

September 27, 1999

Dear Reader,

These diaries are very personal, but I decided that it might help the bereaved parent to read the thoughts of another going through the same. Writing—many times in the middle of the night—was a major tool in working through the disbelief and anger in my path of grief.

As I go to publication, I reflect on how difficult it has been to actually get published. The words "too depressing" were spoken often by publishers and editors. They appeared to want a happy ending, where there can be none, to this non-fiction writing.

I strove to give hope for a future and to validate the incredibly painful path this is for a bereaved mom, not to draw a pretty or untrue picture. Details for each person may differ, but the overall despair and pain is similar.

If, in reading this book, you feel the hope that we bereaved work so hard to gain, or as a non-bereaved parent you understand a little better what it is like for us, then I have succeeded.

My fellow bereaved parent, my heart goes with you.

Terri

ABOUT THE AUTHOR

Terri & John Huber

Terri Huber is a wife, mother, homemaker and businesswoman residing in Tigard, Oregon for the last twenty-five years. This is her first venture into the field of writing.

John Huber is a husband, father, businessman and wonderful poet. He and Terri have been married twenty-eight years.